高职高专实用英语教程

国家林业和草原局职业教育"十三五"规划教材
全国生态文明信息化遴选融合出版项目

主　编　连　颖
副主编　丁　磊

中国林业出版社

图书在版编目（CIP）数据

高职高专实用英语教程/连颖主编. -- 北京：中国林业出版社，2021.8
国家林业和草原局职业教育"十三五"规划教材
ISBN 978-7-5219-0985-2

Ⅰ.①高… Ⅱ.①连… Ⅲ.①英语—高等职业教育—教材 Ⅳ.①H319.39

中国版本图书馆CIP数据核字(2021)第017495号

国家林业和草原局职业教育"十三五"规划教材
全国生态文明信息化遴选融合出版项目

课程信息

中国林业出版社

策划编辑：吴　卉　孙源璞
责任编辑：张　佳　孙源璞
电　　话：010-83143561
邮　　箱：books@theways.cn
小途教育：http://edu.cfph.net

出版发行：中国林业出版社
邮　　编：100009
地　　址：北京西城区德内大街刘海胡同7号
印　　刷：河北京平诚乾印刷有限公司
版　　次：2021年8月第1版
印　　次：2021年8月第1次
字　　数：330千字
开　　本：787mm×1092mm　1/16
印　　张：14.25
定　　价：48.00元

凡本书出现缺页、倒页、脱页等问题，请向出版社图书营销中心调换
版权所有　侵权必究

《高职高专实用英语教程》
编写人员

主　　编：连　颖

副 主 编：丁　磊

参编人员：赵义莲　郑佳佳　苏靖辉　陈紫娟

前 言
PREFACE

一、简介

《高职高专实用英语教程》是一本结合职业教育英语教学特点，针对高职高专学生程度，按照中高职衔接、专升本衔接的理念设计的教材。

本教材是供高职高专大学一年级使用的公共基础课英语教材，共有 9 个单元，可供一个学期的教学使用，每个单元配有教学 PPT 和扩展内容，可扫码查看。

二、编写理念

1. 中高职衔接，专升本衔接

本教材根据职业教育人才培养的要求，参考《中等职业学校英语教学大纲》《普通高中英语课程标准》《高等职业教育英语课程教学要求（试行）》《高职高专升本科英语水平测试》的要求，在教材设计上做到衔接有度，逻辑清晰。

2. 以学生为主，教师为辅

本教材充分体现以学生为学习主体，以大学生学习特点和认知方法为导向，依照学生英语基础，注重综合素质培养，培养学生日常交际的英语应用能力，以拓宽学生的国际视野为最终教学目的。

3. 注重职业性和实践性

职业教育以突出职业性和实践性为主，本教材突出职业性和实践性，在最大范围内提高学生的综合素质、满足学生今后的专业发展。以教育部对高职高专院校"产、学、研"相结合培养内容为依据，特别强调"加强英语语言基础和基本技能的同时，重视培养学生使用英语进行交际的能力"的要求，我们积极探索对英语"理论够用，听懂会说，应用熟练"的教学模式，为学生正确使用英语词汇、语法奠定坚实的基础，力求编写出既能符合大学英语课程体系、课程内容的教学改革要求，又能适应高职高专教学的教材。

三、教材特色

1. 关注学生英语基础，凸显高职英语教学的实用性

本教材适应高职学生的英语基础，所有对话和阅读的选题及内容都充分考虑到学生的实际英语水平、年龄特点以及今后的职业能力发展需求，活动设计层层铺垫，语言输入量大且注重学生的参与及互动，既能调动学生学习积极性，又能有效培养学生在职场环境下运用语言的能力。

2. 教学设计循序渐进，符合语言学习规律

本教材每个单元以"主题""拓展阅读""语法"作为三维支撑体系，从对话到知识拓展再到巩固语法知识，循序渐进，将话题、场景、任务、语法等学习要素有机结合，符合语言学习规律，培养学生在职场环境下的综合语言应用能力。

3. 内容新颖、有创意

教材的编写既照顾到学生的实际英语水平，又重在应用能力的进一步提高。同时，每个单元设计的拓展内容有效融入课程思政、创新创业、中华传统文化、森林文化知识。多元文化知识有效帮助学生开拓视野，增长知识，提高跨文化交际意识。

4. 多维资源体系，操作性强

本教材包含学生用书（含练习及答案），教学 PPT 及课外拓展阅读材料。内容丰富，层次多样，可以满足不同程度学生的需求。

四、单元结构

本教材单元内容强调真实任务和语言运用，设计了情景对话、拓展阅读、跨文化交际案例分析、应用文写作、语法 5 个部分，以满足职场通用交际需求。全书共 3 个模块 9 个单元，其中模块 1 为"结交新朋友"，以会展商务服务为主，模拟结识新客户、行程安排、如何推销产品及商榷等情景展开对话，涵盖 1~4 单元；模块 2 为"创新创业"，围绕当前大学生热门的创新创业展开对话，涵盖 5~7 单元；模块 3 为"森林文化"，响应国家"绿水青山就是金山银山"的生态文明发展理念，围绕森林文化、旅游展开对话，涵盖 8~9 单元。各个教学单元构成及特点如下。

1. 学习目标

本环节体现本单元学习目标，在学习开始前由教师提出，在学习结束后由教师要求学生完成具体任务，体现出任务趋向型的教学理念。

2. 情景对话

本环节围绕单元主题展开，每个单元都有若干个对话。对话设计目的在于通过对话、词汇等提供具体场景和语境，激活学生学习兴趣，围绕话题展开对话训练，提高语言实用性。

3. 拓展阅读

本环节围绕情景对话场景中关键词展开阅读，此部分重点在"丰富"学生的知识面，对于学有余力的学生还可以扫描书中二维码，查阅相关的课外资料。本教材中所节选的文段均为社会热点问题，和大学生生活息息相关，能有效激发学生的学习兴趣。

4. 跨文化交际

语言作为文化的载体，在国际交往中意义重要。本教材每个单元均嵌入跨文化交际内容，是为了拓宽大学生的国际视野，使他们了解外国文化知识，认识中西方文化差异，以便更好地进行国际交流。

5. 实用写作

本环节是本教材的职业性和实践性相结合的体现，在阅读的基础上，选取了与本单元主题相关的实用文体，包括邀请函、传真、电子邮件、申请信、通知、请假条、推荐信和备忘录等。了解应用文体的写作特点、完成写作任务，有针对性地培养学生现实生活中运用英语的能力。

6. 语法

本环节为本教材的重点特色之一。高职学生英语基础薄弱，有些学生专升本的愿望强烈，但是学习英语又无从下手。针对这种情况，本教材遵循"够用主义"，将英语语法进行梳理简化，从基本语法教起，知识点涵盖初高中基本语法，能满足基础薄弱的学生的需求。每个单元还配有专门的练习，讲练结合，注重实效。

7. 二维码

本环节是针对学习兴趣高、程度好的学生设计的，学生只需扫一扫每个单元最后所印二维码，即可获得相关阅读材料，让学习者在学有余力的情况下，拓展知识面。

8. 日常用语

本环节的内容主要是一些英语谚语以及英语常用口语，可以在教师与学生的课堂互动中活跃气氛，是为提高学生的英语实际应用能力而设计的环节。

五、教学建议

本教材适合高职高专一年级在校生，或者具有一定英语基础的学习者使用，也可作为专升本学生的复习考试用书。本书共9个单元，建议一学期使用（32~36学时）完成教学任务，每3~4节课完成一个单元学习。

六、编写队伍

《高职高专实用英语教程》教材由福建林业职业技术学院连颖副教授担任主编，福建林业职业技术学院丁磊老师担任副主编，编写组成员有赵义莲、苏靖辉、郑佳佳、陈紫娟。其中，连颖老师负责单元1、2、3、4、5；丁磊老师负责单元6、7、8；赵义莲老师老师单元9；苏靖辉、陈紫娟老师负责教学PPT制作；郑佳佳老师负责跨文化交际内容的审定；全书由连颖老师审定。本书的编写人员均是长期从事于教学一线的专任教师，有着丰富的教学实践经验，能够保证教材编写的科学性、针对性以及实践性。在编写过程中，感谢邓建琼、张应梅老师的支持和建议。本书在编写的过程中参考了多方面的资料，编者在此对所用资料的作者表示衷心的感谢。由于水平有限，书中有疏漏和不足在所难免，恳请广大读者不吝批评指正。

编者

2021年5月

目 录
CONTENTS

Preface

Module 1 Meeting New Friends

Unit 1   Meeting New People in a Trade Fair ················· 002

Learning Objectives ··002
Section Ⅰ   Dialogues ··002
Section Ⅱ   Extensive Reading ··008
Section Ⅲ   Case Analysis in Intercultural Communication ···············013
Section Ⅳ   Practical Writing: Invitation Letter ·······················014
Section Ⅴ   Grammar: Noun（名词）····································016

Unit 2   Making Travel Arrangements ························· 024

Learning Objectives ··024
Section Ⅰ   Dialogues ··024
Section Ⅱ   Extensive Reading ··031
Section Ⅲ   Case Analysis in Intercultural Communication ···············037
Section Ⅳ   Practical Writing: Fax ····································038
Section Ⅴ   Grammar: Adjective & Adverb（形容词及副词）··············039

Unit 3   Promoting the Products ···························· 048

Learning Objectives ··048
Section Ⅰ   Dialogues ··048

Section Ⅱ	Extensive Reading ··· 054
Section Ⅲ	Case Analysis in Intercultural Communication ···················· 060
Section Ⅳ	Practical Writing: Letter of Thanks ····································· 061
Section Ⅴ	Grammar: Verb（动词）·· 063

Unit 4　Business Negotiation ··· 071

Learning Objectives ·· 071
Section Ⅰ	Dialogues ·· 071
Section Ⅱ	Extensive Reading ·· 077
Section Ⅲ	Case Analysis in Intercultural Communication ···················· 086
Section Ⅳ	Practical Writing: Letter of Application ····························· 086
Section Ⅴ	Grammar: Preposition（介词）··· 089

Module 2　Innovation and Entrepreneurship

Unit 5　Innovation ··· 096

Learning Objectives ·· 096
Section Ⅰ	Dialogues ·· 096
Section Ⅱ	Extensive Reading ·· 101
Section Ⅲ	Case Analysis in Intercultural Communication ···················· 107
Section Ⅳ	Practical Writing: Post ··· 108
Section Ⅴ	Grammar: Sentences Constituents & Main Structures（句子成分及主要句型结构）··· 111

Unit 6　Entrepreneurship ··· 118

Learning Objectives ·· 118
Section Ⅰ	Dialogues ·· 118
Section Ⅱ	Extensive Reading ·· 124
Section Ⅲ	Case Analysis in Intercultural Communication ···················· 130
Section Ⅳ	Practical Writing: Notice ·· 131
Section Ⅴ	Grammar: Nominal Clause（名词性从句）··························· 133

Unit 7　Volunteer ·· 140

　　Learning Objectives ·· 140
　　Section Ⅰ　Dialogues ··· 140
　　Section Ⅱ　Extensive Reading ·· 146
　　Section Ⅲ　Case Analysis in Intercultural Communication ··························· 153
　　Section Ⅳ　Practical Writing: Letter of Recommendation ···························· 154
　　Section Ⅴ　Grammar: Attributive Clause（定语从句）································ 156

Module 3　The Culture of the Forest

Unit 8　Mountain Trip ·· 166

　　Learning Objectives ·· 166
　　Section Ⅰ　Dialogues ··· 166
　　Section Ⅱ　Extensive Reading ·· 172
　　Section Ⅲ　Case Analysis in Intercultural Communication ··························· 178
　　Section Ⅳ　Practical Writing: Written Request for a Leave ·························· 180
　　Section Ⅴ　Grammar: Adverbial Clause（状语从句）································· 182

Unit 9　Forest Protection ··· 190

　　Learning Objectives ·· 190
　　Section Ⅰ　Dialogues ··· 190
　　Section Ⅱ　Extensive Reading ·· 196
　　Section Ⅲ　Case Analysis in Intercultural Communication ··························· 202
　　Section Ⅳ　Practical Writing: Memo ·· 203
　　Section Ⅴ　Grammar: Non-finite Verb（非谓语动词）······························· 205

REFERENCES ··· 213

1

Module 1
Meeting New Friends

Unit 1

Meeting New People in a Trade Fair

扫一扫查看
本章教学PPT

Learning Objectives

【About Knowledge】

1. To break the ice with strangers in a trade fair.
2. To invite a foreign company to a trade fair.
3. To invite customers to a dinner.
4. To know more about the noun.

【About Skills】

To write an invitation letter.

Section I *Dialogues*

Dialogue 1

Inviting a New Customer

Ms. Li, the marketing manager from China Shenzhen Foreign Trade (Group) Co. Ltd., calls a new customer, Mr. Ryan from a foreign trade company, to **attend** *their fair.*

Ms. Li: Good morning. This is Ms. Li from China Shenzhen Foreign Trade (Group) Co. Ltd. Is that Mr. Ryan speaking?

Mr. Ryan: Yes, may I help you?

Ms. Li: I'm calling to **invite** you to attend the 128th China Import & Export **Commodities**

Fair from October 31st to November 4th, 2020. We're one of the manufacturers **specialized** in Men's PU and leather shoes, including sandals, casual shoes and children's shoes. Our products are both in high quality and **reasonable** price. It would be a great pleasure to meet you at the **exhibition**.

Mr. Ryan: We accept it with pleasure.

Ms. Li: We will publish a special edition about the products on the show with the link to the official website of our company at the same time, and send you a copy by e-mail.

Mr. Ryan: I **appreciate** that very much.

Ms. Li: By the way, I'll fax you the application form and other necessary information you need very soon.

Mr. Ryan: Thank you! See you.

Ms. Li: **Looking forward to** seeing you in the fair.

Vocabulary and notes

1. attend: v. to go to or be present at an event；出席；参加

2. invite: v. to ask somebody politely to come or go somewhere, or ask somebody to do something；邀请。搭配：v. + n. invite attention; invite company; invite trouble; invite challenge

3. commodity: n. an item that is bought and sold, especially an unprocessed material；商品；日用品

4. specialize：v. to devote time exclusively to an interest, skill, or field of study；专门从事。搭配：specialize in + n. 专门从事……

5. reasonable: adj. acceptable and according to common sense or normal practice；合理的；明智的

6. exhibition: n. a public display, usually for a limited period, of a collection of works of art or objects of special interest；展览会；展览品

7. appreciate: v. to recognize and like the qualities in somebody or something；欣赏；感激

8. look forward to: v. to anticipate a future event with excitement or pleasure；盼望；期待

9. We're one of the manufacturers specialized in Men's PU and leather shoes, including sandals, cusual shoes and children's shoes. 我们是一家专业生产 PU 材质和皮质男式鞋的制造商，生产的产品包括凉鞋、休闲鞋和童鞋。

Dialogue 2

Meeting New People in a Trade Fair

Mr. Ryan, an American from a foreign trade company, arrived at the Canton Fair for the first time. He met Mr. Wang, Ms. Li's colleague, in the booth.

Ms. Li: I would like to introduce Mr. Wang, the marketing department manager of our company.

Mr. Wang: Nice to meet you, Mr. Ryan.

Mr. Ryan: Nice to meet you, too, Mr. Wang.

Mr. Wang: Welcome to Guangzhou. Is it your first time to visit the Canton fair?

Mr. Ryan: Yes, it's my first time to visit Guangzhou and the Canton fair. Guangzhou is a very beautiful city.

Mr. Wang: Thank you. Guangzhou is the largest city in southern China. It's so big and marvelous that most of the visitors do not have enough time to enjoy it. I wish you a pleasant stay here.

Mr. Ryan: May I have the honor to see the samples newly issued by your company?

Mr. Wang: The honor is mine. Look at this pair of shoes, our new arrival. It looks smart and perfectly fit for young people. That pair, our classic style, is very elegant. It has different colors for options. And I will show you around our factory nearby tomorrow.

Mr. Ryan: I appreciate you taking the time.

Mr. Wang: Don't mention it. I hope you'll have a pleasant journey here.

Vocabulary and notes

1. Canton Fair: 广州交易会

2. booth: n. a tent, stall, or other light structure at a fair or exhibition, offering some form of entertainment or goods for sale；展位

3. marvelous: adj. extraordinarily wonderful；妙极的；了不起的

4. sample: n. a small amount or part of something, used as an example of the character, features, or quality of the whole；样品

5. new arrival: n. something that has recently arrived somewhere；新品

6. smart: adj. fashionable and stylish；时尚的

7. option: n. a choice that is or can be taken, especially a course of action that remains open for somebody to choose；选项

Dialogue 3

Inviting Customers to a Dinner

Ms. Li is inviting her customer, Mr. Ryan, to a dinner.

Mr. Ryan: Hello.

Ms. Li: Hello, is that Mr. Ryan?

Mr. Ryan: Yes.

Ms. Li: This is Ms. Li. How are you?

Mr. Ryan: Not too bad, thanks. And you?

Ms. Li: Fine. Are you free on Tuesday night? I'd like to invite you to a dinner.

Mr. Ryan: I'm terribly sorry, but I've already made an **arrangement** for Tuesday.

Ms. Li: That's a pity. How about Wednesday?

Mr. Ryan: That would be fine.

Ms. Li: Great. What time would you like to meet?

Mr. Ryan: Whenever is **suitable** for you. I have no plans for that day.

Ms. Li: OK, let's say 6 pm.

Mr. Ryan: And where would you like to meet?

Ms. Li: I can **pick** you **up** at the gate of your company. Also, what type of food do you like?

Mr. Ryan: I'm not very familiar with Chinese **cuisine**. What would you **recommend**?

Ms. Li: Well, have you heard of Beijing Roast Duck? It's a local **specialty**.

Mr. Ryan: Of course! Beijing Roast Duck is world-famous. I would love to try it.

Ms. Li: OK, let's have that then.

Mr. Ryan: All right. Well, I'll see you later.

Ms. Li: See you later, goodbye.

Mr. Ryan: Bye.

Vocabulary and notes

1. arrangement: n. something that has to be done so that something else can happen in the future, or the making of such preparations；安排；筹划；布置；协议

2. suitable: adj. of the right type or quality for a particular purpose or occasion；合适的；适当的

3. pick…up: v. to stop a vehicle and let a passenger or passengers in；开车接送

4. cuisine: n. the food you can eat in a particular place, especially a restaurant or hotel；菜肴；烹饪；烹调法

5. recommend: v. to suggest something as worthy of being accepted, used, or done；推荐；介绍；劝告；建议

6. specialty: n. a food or drink prepared in a special way that a person, a restaurant, or a region is well known for and that you cannot always get in other places；招牌菜；专业；专长

Dialogue 4

Providing Attendance Information

Chen Lan (Ms. Chen), an assistant of the trade fair, is giving attendance information to Ms. Li on the phone.

Ms. Chen: Good morning, Organizing Committee of Chinese Import and Export Commodities Fair. What can I do for you?

Ms. Li: Good morning, I'm the sales manager of Yangguang Computer Company. I'd like to know something about your exhibition in April.

Ms. Chen: Well, the exhibition is about to open on April 15th. We have two phases for different commodities. The attendance will be the largest ever because we have received *registrations* for the exhibition from many factories and *enterprises* and we *expect* to have about 2000 professional buying groups from 150 countries and regions.

Ms. Li: Are there any booths still *available*?

Ms. Chen: Yes, we still have some *vacant* booths. I would advise you to book right away before they are all gone.

Ms. Li: How about the price for a booth?

Ms. Chen: The average price of a **standard** booth is USD2,600, but the price **varies** according to the size and location.

Ms. Li: Could we have some discounts?

Ms. Chen: Of course. We will give you a good discount if you **sign up** now.

Ms. Li: Thank you. We'll sign up now. And the deposit will be credited to your account in a few days. As for the exact booth, we will phone back to talk it over.

Ms. Chen: OK. I will be sure to recommend some good ones to you.

Vocabulary and notes

1. assistant: n. someone whose job is to help another person in their work, for example by doing the easier parts of it；助理；助教；店员

2. attendance: n. an instance of being at an event, or the practice of regularly going to a school, church, or other institution；出席 (attend 的名词)

3. registration: n. the act or an instance of registering somebody or something, or the process of being registered；登记；注册

4. enterprise: n. a commercial company；企业；单位

5. expect: v. to wait for, or look forward to, something that is believed to be going to happen or arrive；期待

6. available: adj. not too busy to do something；有空的

7. vacant: adj. If something is vacant, it is not being used by anyone；空的

8. standard: adj. constituting or not differing from the norm；普通的；常规的；n. 标准

9. vary: v. to change within a range of possibilities, or in connection with something else, or make something undergo such a change；变化

10. sign up: v. to agree to participate in something, or get somebody to agree to participate in something, especially by way of a signature；报名

Activity

Make up a dialogue based on the following situation.

Suppose you are an assistant of the 128th China Import & Export Commodities Fair. You are calling one of your regular customers to invite him to attend the trade fair from Oct. 15th to 20th.

Action is the proper fruit of knowledge. 行动是知识的巧果。

Section II Extensive Reading

Passage 1

Introduction of China Import and Export Fair (Canton Fair)

China Import and Export Fair, also known as the Canton Fair, was established in 1957, **co-hosted** by the Ministry of Commerce of P. R. C. and the People's Government of Guangdong Province and organized by China Foreign Trade Centre, which is held every spring and autumn in Guangzhou, China. Canton Fair is a **comprehensive** international trading event which has the longest history, the largest scale, the most complete exhibit variety, the largest buyer attendance and the greatest business turnover in China.

After 63 years' reform and innovative development, the Canton Fair has **withstood various challenges** and never been suspended. The Canton Fair not only **enhances** the trade connection between China and the world, but also **demonstrates** China's image and developing achievements. The Canton Fair is an outstanding platform for Chinese enterprises to explore the international market, The Canton Fair **serves as** the first and foremost platform to **promote** China's foreign trade, and a barometer of the foreign trade sector, which is the window and symbol of China's opening up.

Up to the 126th session, the accumulated export volume has **amounted to** about USD 1.4126 trillion and the total number of overseas buyers has reached 8.99 million. The exhibition area of one session totals 1.185 million m^2 and the number of exhibitors from home and abroad stands at nearly 25,000. In each session, about 200,000 buyers attend the Fair from more than 210 countries and regions all over the world.

On the opening of the 120th Canton Fair in October, 2016, Chinese President Xi Jinping sent a congratulatory letter. In the letter, President Xi **affirmed** the Canton Fair's important status and contributions in China's reform and opening policies and eco-social development, pointing out the focus and direction of the Canton Fair in the new period, which are of great significance to further expanding the opening-up, and **cultivating** new advantages in foreign trade competition.

At present, under the guidance of **Xi Jinping's Thought on Socialism with Chinese Characteristics for a New Era**, Canton Fair will uphold the development principles of innovation, coordination, green development, opening up and sharing, pushing forward the system innovation and business mode, and improving the specialization, informatization, marketization, and internationalization of the Canton Fair. We are **endeavored** to build a "Smart Canton Fair" and "Green Canton Fair". We are working hard to transform Canton Fair from an export trading platform to a comprehensive one-integrating customer networking, display and negotiation, industrial exchange, information release and product promotion. We are working hard to transform Canton Fair from an export trading platform to a comprehensive platform which incorporates customer networking, display and negotiation, industrial exchange, information release and product promotion. We will give full play to Canton Fair's function as an overall platform for opening-up and make new contributions to China's development into a strong economic and trade power and the development of open economy.

（来源：https://www.cantonfair.org.cn/）

Vocabulary and notes

1. co-host: 联合主办

2. comprehensive: adj. covering many things or a wide area；广泛的

3. withstand various challenges: 经受住了各种挑战

4. enhance: v. to increase the clarity, degree of detail, or another quality of an electronic image by using a computer program；增强

5. demonstrate: v. to show or prove something clearly and convincingly；表明

6. serve as: v. 作为；充当

7. promote: v. to encourage the growth and development of something；促进

8. amount to: v. to come to a total when added up；合计

9. affirm: v. to state firmly or publicly that something is true；证明；证实

10. cultivate: v. to improve or develop something, usually by study or education；培养

11. Xi Jinping's Thought on Socialism with Chinese Characteristics for a New Era: 习近平新时代中国特色社会主义思想

12. endeavor: v. to try very hard to do something；尽力

13. Canton Fair is a comprehensive international trading event which has the longest history, the largest scale, the most complete exhibit variety, the largest buyer attendance and the greatest business turnover in China. 广交会是中国历史最悠久、规模最大、展品品种最齐全、买家出席人数最多、成交额最大的综合性国际贸易盛会。

14. In the letter, President Xi affirmed the Canton Fair's important status and contributions in China's reform and opening policies and eco-social development, pointing out the focus and direction of the Canton Fair in the new period, which are of great significance to further expanding the opening-up, and cultivating new advantages in foreign trade competition. 习主席在信中肯定了广交会在我国改革开放和生态社会发展中的重要地位和贡献，指出了新时期广交会的工作重点和方向，对进一步扩大对外开放，培育外贸竞争新优势具有重要意义。

 译文

中国进出口商品交易会（广交会）介绍

中国进出口商品交易会，又称广交会，成立于1957年。由中华人民共和国商务部和广东省人民政府共同主办，中国对外贸易中心承办，每年春秋两季在广州举办。广交会是中国历史最悠久、规模最大、展品品种最全、买家出席人数最多、成交额最大的综合性国际贸易盛会。

经过63年的改革创新发展，广交会经受住了各种挑战，从未停办过。广交会不仅增进了中国与世界的贸易联系，而且展示了中国的形象和发展成就。广交会是中国企业开拓国际市场的优秀平台，是促进中国对外贸易的首要平台，也是外贸领域的晴雨表，是中国对外开放的窗口和标志。

截至第126届会议，累计出口额约14126万亿美元，海外采购商总数达899万人次。一届展览面积118.5万平方米，国内外参展商近2.5万人。在每届展会上，来自全球210多个国家和地区约20万名买家出席展会。

在2016年10月的第120届广交会开幕式上，习近平主席发出了贺信。习主席在信中肯定了广交会在我国改革开放和生态社会发展中的重要地位和贡献，指出了新时期广交会的工作重点和方向，对进一步扩大对外开放，培育外贸竞争新优势具有重要意义。

当前，广交会将以习近平新时代中国特色社会主义思想为指导，坚持创新、协调、绿色发展、开放共享的发展方针，推进体制创新和商业模式创新，提高专业化、信息化水平，广交会的市场化、国际化。我们致力于打造"智慧广交会"和"绿色广交会"。我们正在努力将广交会从一个出口贸易平台转变为集客户网络、展示洽谈、产业交流、信息发布、产品推广为一体的综合性平台。我们正在努力将广交会从一个出口贸易平台转变为集客户网络、展示洽谈、产业交流、信息发布、产品推广为一体的综合性平台。充分发挥广交会对外开放的总体平台作用，为我国建设经贸强国、发展开放型经济作出新贡献。

Passage 2

History of Exhibition

The exhibition activities of human society **originated from** the sacrificial activities of primitive（原始）society in the primitive stage. The exhibitions that directly used agricultural and animal products and handicraft products as **display** means could be called sacrificial goods exhibition. Later, there was religious art exhibition, and then it developed to the commodity display and sales of ancient goods trading fairs. The ancient world exhibition stage is from the 8th to 16th century AD known as the ancient market and temple fair. The European fairs had a relatively concentrated scale, a long holding cycle, and relatively complete functions: retail, wholesale, international trade, culture and entertainment. The champagne market, the most famous international trade fair in France, was particularly important in the 12th—13th century, which was established by a French Champagne Earl and held in turn in four cities in his **territory**, becoming the place of gathering for businessmen from France, Italy, Germany and Britain. The formation and development of champagne market was the result of social division of labor and the development of productive forces. It was a relatively perfect form of ancient exhibition activities.

The modern world exhibition is from 17th to 19th century. During this period, European exhibitions had revolutionary changes, including pure art exhibition and pure **propaganda** national industrial exhibition. The Great Exhibition of Industry of All Nations in 1851 is a **milestone** in the history of world exhibitions. At that time, the industrial revolution made Britain the "factory of the world". In order to show its strong national strength to the world, Britain held this **unprecedented** grand event, which lasted five months and attracted more than 6 million visitors. This marked the discovery of a new form of large-scale international civilization exchange. This kind of exhibition gradually developed into a unique exhibition reflecting human science and technology and culture — World Expo. The "world industrial exposition" in Britain is regarded as the first World Exhibition in the world. Since then, the world exposition has been held every two years and continued to this day. Every Expo is a vivid **encyclopedia**. Over the past century and a half, the World Expo has solemnly introduced the world's first important inventions: Bell Telephone and gramophone at Philadelphia World Expo in 1876, TV set at New York World Expo in 1939, electronic computer technology and copier at New York World

Expo in 1964, robot technology at Tsukuba Expo in 1985, *etc*. There are more than 1000 kinds of newly developed products in the award reports submitted by previous World Expos, which record the progress of human **conquering** nature, increasing productivity and improving quality of life, which can be called a milestone in human history.

The contemporary world exhibition emerges in form of trade exhibitions and becomes an important channel for product circulation. During the two World Wars, comprehensive trade exhibitions developed rapidly into the dominant form. After the Second World War, trade exhibitions have developed rapidly towards specialization, becoming a huge and complete system.

Vocabulary and notes

1. originate from: v. 起源于

2. display: n. a collection of things arranged or done for others to see, especially something considered attractive, interesting, or entertaining；展示

3. territory: n. land, or an area of land；领土

4. propaganda: n. information put out by an organization or government to promote a policy, idea, or cause；宣传

5. milestone: n. a significant or important event, in the history of a country or in somebody's life；里程碑

6. unprecedented: adj. having no earlier parallel or equivalent；史无前例的

7. encyclopedia: n. a reference work offering comprehensive information on all or specialized areas of knowledge；百科全书

8. conquer: v. to be victorious；战胜

9. The exhibitions that directly used agricultural and animal products and handicraft products as display means could be called sacrificial goods exhibition. 直接以展示农畜产品和手工艺品为手段的展览，可以称为祭祀品展览。

10. The "world industrial exposition" in Britain is regarded as the first World Exhibition in the world. Since then, the world exposition has been held every two years and continued to this day. 英国的"世界工业博览会"被认为是世界上第一个世界性的展览会。从那时起，世界博览会每两年举办一次，一直持续到今天。

译文

展览会历史

人类社会的展示活动起源于原始社会的祭祀活动。直接以展示农畜产品和手工艺品为手段的展览，可以称为祭祀品展览。后来有了宗教艺术展览，再发展到商品展示和古代商品交易会的销售。古代世界展览的舞台是公元 8~16 世纪的古代集市和庙会。欧洲博览会规模相对集中，举办周期长，功能相对完整：零售、批发、国际贸易、文化娱乐等。香槟市场是法国最著名的国际贸易博览会，在 12~13 世纪尤为重要，它是由一位法国香槟伯爵创办，在其境内的四个城市轮流举办，成为法国、意大利、德国和英国商人的聚集地。香槟市场的形成和发展是社会分工和生产力发展的结果。这是一种比较完善的古代展览活动形式。

现代世界展览是从 17 世纪到 19 世纪。在这一时期，欧洲的展览发生了革命性的变化，包括纯粹的艺术展览和纯粹的宣传性国家工业展览。1851 年世界各国工业大展是世界展览史上的里程碑。当时，工业革命使英国成为"世界工厂"。为了向世界展示其强大的国力，英国举办了这一史无前例的盛会，历时 5 个月，吸引了 600 多万游客。这标志着一种新的大规模国际文明交流形式的出现。这种展览逐渐发展成为反映人类科技文化的独特展览——世博会。英国的"世界工业博览会"被认为是世界上第一个世界性的展览会。从那时起，世界博览会每两年举办一次，一直持续到今天。每一届世博会都是一部生动的百科全书。在过去的一个半世纪里，世博会隆重地介绍了世界上最早的重要发明：1876 年费城世博会的电话和留声机、1939 年纽约世博会的电视机、1964 年纽约世博会的电子计算机技术和复印机、1985 年筑波博览会的机器人技术等。历届世博会提交的获奖报告中有 1000 多种新开发产品，记录了人类征服自然、提高生产力、提高生活质量的进程，堪称人类历史上的里程碑。

当代世界博览会以贸易展览的形式出现，成为商品流通的重要渠道。两次世界大战期间，综合性贸易展览和博览会迅速发展成为主导形式。二战后，贸易展览迅速向专业化方向发展，成为一个庞大而完整的体系。

Section III *Case Analysis in Intercultural Communication*

Greeting: Have you had your lunch? / Where are you going?

When I first went to Hong Kong a number of years ago, I had no idea about the Chinese language or the Chinese culture. Shortly after my arrival, I went to the bank on my way to school. I was extremely surprised when the bank clerk asked me if I had had my lunch. In British culture, this question would be regarded as an indirect invitation to lunch, and between unmarried young people, it indicates a young man's interest in dating a girl. Since he was a complete stranger, I was quite taken aback. I proceeded to school and was even more surprised when one of the teachers asked me the same question.

By now I realized that it could not be an invitation, but I was puzzled as to why they kept asking it. In the following days, as I was asked the question again and again, I came to the conclusion that people must be concerned about my health. I was somewhat underweight, and I assumed they must be worried that I was not eating properly. Only later, did I find out that the question had no real significance at all, it was merely a greeting.

English people have a very strong sense of privacy. They are easily offended by comments which seem to invade their personal lives, so the Chinese greeting "where are you going? " is uncomfortable to them. They regard it as a request for information and as an invasion of their privacy. In fact, many foreign teachers in China have complained that their room attendants are spies because the attendants have greeted them with "where are you going?"

Question for discussion

How would the Westerners greet each other?

分析：中国人打招呼经常问对方："上哪去？""吃过了没有？""最近忙什么？"等。而西方人打招呼一般用："Hello""Hi""Good morning/afternoon/evening""How do you do""Nice to meet you"等。对中国人关怀式的问候，西方人会误认为是干涉他的个人私事。

Section Ⅳ *Practical Writing: Invitation Letter*

邀请信函在形式上大体分为两种：

1. 正规的格式（formal），亦称请柬；

2. 非正式格式（informal），即一般的邀请函。

邀请函在形式上不如请柬那样正规，但也很考究，书写时应将邀请的时间（年、月、日、钟点）、地点、场合写清楚。

Sample

Dear Mr.Li,

　　ABC Computer Software Corporation is planning a dinner party to celebrate its 15th anniversary. The party will be held at 6:30 pm. on May 20th, 2016, Friday in the Hilton Hotel.

　　You are my good friend, and we have already had many years of cooperation. To express my heartfelt thanks for your support and understanding, I sincerely invite you to come and spend the time with me.

　　I do hope you can make it. I am looking forward with great pleasure to seeing you.

　　Sincerely yours,

John Smith
Manager

Useful expressions

1. I am pleased to invite you to attend…

   非常高兴邀请你参加……

2. It is my pleasure/a great honor for me to invite you to…

   非常荣幸邀请你参加……

3. It is with great pleasure that I invite you to attend…

   非常高兴邀请你参加……

4. I take great pleasure in inviting you to…

   非常高兴邀请你参加……

5. I am longing to see you soon.

   我期待早点见到你。

6. I am sure that you will enjoy yourself here.

   我保证你会高兴到这儿来。

7. We look forward to seeing you.

   期待你的到来。

8. I hope that you won't decline my invitation.

   我希望你不要拒绝我的邀请。

Practice

November 1st, 2011

Dear Anna,

We are planning a party to _____
（庆祝弗兰德四十岁生日）. It will be held at 6:00 p. m. _____
_____ （下周一，11月7日）in the Sunward Fishery Restaurant.

I do hope you can come. _____
（我非常高兴地期待着）to seeing you.

_____（谨启）

Section Ⅴ Grammar: Noun（名词）

一、名词的概念

名词是表示人物、地方、国家、动物或物品等名称的词。

```
          ┌ 物质名词：表示无法分为个体的实物，如：air        ┐
          │ 抽象名词：表示性质、状态、品质、情感等没有实     │ 不可数名词
    ┌ 普通名词 ┤           物的名词，如：fear（恐惧）、beauty（美 ├
    │        │           丽）、illness（疾病）、courage（勇气）│
    │        │ 个体名词：表示某类人或东西中的个体，如：gun   ┐
名词 ┤        └ 集体名词：表示一群人或一些物的名词，如：family ├ 可数名词
    │                   （家庭）、people（人民）、class（班）、cattle（牛）┘
    │
    └ 专有名词：一般表示人名、地名、物品、团体、机构和事件等特有的名称。如：
              Tom（汤姆）、Sunday（周日）、the Great wall（长城）、February（二月）
```

可数名词：能表示为类似一个鸡蛋等具体概念的，要用名词单数或复数形式。表示名词的单数时，要在名词的前面加冠词 a 或 an，如：an egg（一个鸡蛋），a pen（一只钢笔）；表示一个以上时要用复数形式，如：five pens（5支钢笔）(a、an、a few、many、several 等这些与数量有关的词常用来描述可数名词的数量，如：a few books（几本书），several bags 几个袋子）。

不可数名词：不能用不定冠词 a 或 an，也没有复数形式，如液体和肉类：flour（面粉），rice（大米），paper（纸），bread（面包），money（钱）。如想将不可数名词具体时，要用量词，如 a bottle of milk（一瓶牛奶），a glass of water（一杯水）。

名词复数形式：表示一个以上的数目。泛指时用 a、an、one，但表达准确数目时要用 one，而不用 an、one，如 How many sandwiches would you like?（你想要多少块三明治？）I would like just one sandwich.（我只要一块三明治。）比较 May I have a sandwich? 和 May I have one sandwich? 的区别。

二、名词的所有格

名词的所有格表示名词之间的所有关系，有两种表示形式，一种是在名词后加 's；另一种是用 of，表示"……的"。

（1）有生命名词的所有格，如果是单数名词，则加 's，如：Mary's car。如果是以 s 结尾的复数名词，则只在 s 后面加 '，如：teachers' offices。如果是不以 s 结尾的复数名词，则加 's，如：children's palace。组合名词的所有格一般是在最后一个词尾加 's，如：

girlfriend—girlfriend's

someone else—someone else's

a week or three—a week or three's

① 一般词的所有格，直接在词尾加 's；如：Mr. Mott's robot, children's clothes。

② 以 s 结尾的名词所有格只在词尾加 '；如：Teachers' Day。

③ 两人共有的物体，则在第二个名词后加 's；如果分别是两人所有，则在每个名词后面加 's。如：Lucy and Lily's room（指两人共住一个房间），Mrs Green's and Mrs Brown's son（指两人各自的儿子）。

（2）无生命名词的所有格一般用 of 结构。但是 's 形式的所有格可用于以下无生命的名词。表示时间的词：today's newspaper, a twenty minutes' walk, an hour's rest。表示长度或距离的词：three meteres' distance, a boat's length, twenty miles' journey。表示重量的名词：two pounds' weight。表示价格的名词：two dollars' worth；拟人化的名词：Nature's work, nature's lesson（大自然的教训）。国家、机关、团体、城市等机构性名词：the university's library。英文中用定冠词加上形容词表示一类人时应作复数名词，如：the rich（富人），the poor（穷人），the wise（聪明人）。但如果用定冠词加形容词来表示事物则要用作单数名词，如：The beautiful is still here.（美丽的风景依旧）。

① 表示某具体场所时和表示店铺、住所、公共建筑时，所有格后面的名词可省略。

如：the doctor's (office) →the doctor's。

② 名词的定语较长时，有生命的事物也可用 of 短语表示。如：a long story of a 50-year-old man。

③ 双重所有格，如：a friend of his, the big nose of Tom's。

④ 有些表示时间、距离、国家、城市等无生命的东西的名词，也可以加 's 来构成所有格。如：ten minutes' walk, today's newspaper。

（3）名词所有格还可以表示类别。如：a women's college（一所女子学校），the students' book（学生用书）。

（4）还可表示动作名词的执行者，如：the teacher's praise（老师的表扬），the people's shouts（人们的叫喊）。

（5）由 some-, any-, every- 与 -one/-body 结合起来的复合名词，如：someone, everybody 等和 else 连用时，'s 应加在 else 后，如：somebody else's pencil（别人的铅笔）。

（6）双重所有格与 of 的区别。

例：He is a friend of your father's. 他是你父亲的一个朋友。（指其中一个朋友，还有其他朋友）

例：He is a friend of your father. 他是你父亲的朋友。（指强调友好，是朋友，不是同学）

Exercise 1：Singular and Plural Forms of Nouns（名词单复数）

一、单项选择

1. Numerous _____ from the county want to find jobs in this modern city.

 A. youth B. the youths C. youths D. the youth

2. At present, AIDS _____ still an incurable disease.

 A. be B. was C. are D. is

3. Why are your _____ so dirty?

 A. jean B. jeans C. the jeans D. pieces of jeans

4. The crew in the plane _____ large.

 A. had been B. is C. was D. are

5. The scientists want to find two _____.

 A. Man cooks B. man cooks C. Mans cook D. men cooks

6. Most people use their _____.

 A. rights hand B. left hand C. right hands D. left hands

7. Many children want to become _____ so that they can do everything freely.

A. grown-ups   B. growns ups   C. grown-up   D. growns-up

8. Despite well-developed plot the _____ movie could not hold our attention.

A. three-hour   B. three-hours   C. three-hours'   D. three hour

9. These books can give you _____ you need.

A. all the informations   B. all the information
C. informations   D. all of the informations

10. The three little babies are so cute and lovely that they are _____ of fresh air for the whole family.

A. the breath   B. breaths   C. breath   D. a breath

11. Teachers in our school are forced to write eight _____ every year.

A. theses   B. thesis   C. thesises   D. pieces of thesis

12. Her families have taken twelve _____ during the trip.

A. photos   B. photoes   C. photo   D. photoies

13. Look! Eight _____ are playing around in the field.

A. sheeps   B. sheepes   C. sheep   D. shoop

14. He has offered a series of _____ of his writing ability.

A. prooves   B. proof   C. proofs   D. proofes

15. For a banker like Mr. Huang, a donation of one million dollars is nothing but _____ in the ocean.

A. drops   B. drop   C. a drop   D. the drop

16. General Motors _____ many different types of cars each quarter.

A. produce   B. produced   C. have produced   D. produces

17. The play leaves _____ for revision and polish.

A. a small room   B. much room   C. big room   D. many rooms

二、用所给词的适当形式填空

1. Peter, look. There are two _____ (goose) on the lake.

2. We respect and admire all _____ (hero).

3. We find five _____ (knife) in her bag.

4. His brother could hardly live on his _____ (wage).

5. All the _____ (woman doctor) in my hospital got a rise yesterday.

6. Lucy, please send my _____ (regard) to your grandparents.

7. Please give me _____ (ice).

8. We should keep in mind that "no _____ (pain), no gains".

9. She has steak, vegetables, and _____ (fish) for lunch.

10. Guo Jingjing won five _____ (gold medal) in the Olympic Games.

11. Cards _____ (be) not allowed in my home.

12. The police asked three _____ (pass-by) for information about the accident.

13. There are two _____ (piano) in this church.

14. The China Daily _____ (publish) every day.

15. She forgot both of the _____ (room number).

16. He saw that the herd _____ (be) running in all directions.

17. What a pity. Accurate _____ (datum) covering the fact are not obtainable.

18. The news of victory _____ (be) spreading all around.

三、指出并改正错误

1. Due to the development of production, the price of carrot, milk and meat are gradually going down.

2. A large part of the new equipments has been destroyed.

3. Recording machines can encode sounds, pictures, and other informations onto magnetic tape.

4. The better way of looking at a map is not a piece of papers, but as a record of geography.

5. Red deer lives for about 14 years, however, some have been known to live to an age of 22 years.

6. Linguistic does not appeal to my sister as much as math.

7. The committee have announced the final decision.

8. As we all know that cattle provides us with milk and beef.

9. The rest of the water in the pond are polluted.

10. Two hundred Yuan mean a lot to the little boy.

四、翻译

1. 我的家人都是医生。

2. 坏消息是我们没有通过考试。

3. 他和他的哥哥在同一家单位。

4. 篮子里有三个苹果和一个鸡蛋。

Exercise 2: Possessive Case Of Noun（名词所有格）

一、单项选择

1. _____ receives only a small portion of the total amount of sun's energy.

   A The surface of earth   B. The earth's surface

   C. The earth surface   D. The surface earth

2. This is _____ room. The twin sisters share it.

   A. Lucy's and Lily's   B. Lucy's and Lily

   C. Lucy and Lily's   D. Lucy and Lily

3. In _____ time, those bare mountains will be covered with trees.

   A. few years   B. a few years'

   C. a few year   D. a few year's

4. Have you heard the _____ report?

   A. policemen   B. policemen's

   C. policemens'   D. policemens

5. It's about _____ walk from my company.

   A. eleven minute   B. eleven minutes'

   C. eleven minute's   D. eleven minutes

6. —Can I help you?

   —I want _____.

   A. three dollar's worth of pencil   B. three dollars worth of pencil

   C. dollars worth of pencil   D. three dollars-worth pencil

7. Various materials are available to _____.

   A. today of designers   B. today's of designers

   C. today's designers   D today designers

8. She had her hair cut at _____.

   A the barber's   B the barberers

   C the barberd   D the barbers'

9. -How's Lucy's skirt?

   -Her skirt is more beautiful than _____.

   A. her sister's and Kate   B. her sister and Kate

C. her sister and Kate's   D. her sister's and Kate's

10. The two girls always put delicate gifts in _____ stockings on Christmas.

A. each other's   B. each other   C. each others   D. each others'

11. My parents will have a _____ holiday next week. They'll take my brother to Qingdao.

A. ten day's   B. ten days'   C. ten-days   D. ten days

12. I sat between Ted and Ben listening to teacher's lecture . That is to say my seat was between _____.

A. Ted and Ben's   B. Ted's and Ben

C. Ted and Ben   D. Ted's and Ben's

13. It is said that COVID-19 has killed more than _____ people worldwide.

A. ten thousands   B. ten thousands'

C. ten thousand's   D. ten thousand

14. Kelly won the _____ race in the winter sports meeting.

A. 400-metre   B. 400-metres

C. 400 metre   D. 400 metre's

二、用所给词的适当形式填空

1. It's known to all that March 8th is _____ Day. (woman).

2. Taking thirty _____ (minute) exercise every day does good for you.

3. We have to go to _____ (shoe-maker) to get our shoe back.

4. The man over there is my _____ (mother-in-law) brother.

5. It's about an _____ (hour, drive) from here.

6. They gathered at _____ (hotel, entrance).

7. She obtained a _____ (master, degree).

8. Teachers in western countries have a _____ (three months) holiday in a year.

9. She had to go to _____ (her brother) for supper.

10. We watched _____ (movie, Linda).

11. _____ (children, education) presents a big problem.

12. The Wuyi Mountain is one of _____ (Nan Ping) beautiful mountains.

13. It's made from _____ (cow) milk.

14. Without doubt, we can get the final victor, because we have _____ _____ (the support, the people of the whole world).

15. I'll give my English teacher a card for _____ Day. (teacher)

16. She is a good friend of my _____ (mother).

17. _____ (population, country) has increased rapidly.

18. _____ (performance, the doctors) was wonderful.

扫一扫查看
练习参考答案

扫一扫查看
本章拓展资料

Unit 2

Making Travel Arrangements

扫一扫查看
本章教学PPT

Learning Objectives

【About Knowledge】

1. To reserve flight tickets or hotels.
2. To fill in room-reservation forms.
3. To deal with the shipping of exhibits.
4. To get to know more about the adjective and adverb.

【About Skills】

To write a fax.

Section 1 *Dialogues*

Dialogue 1

Contacting the Exhibition Center about Flight and Hotel Details

Mr. Ryan, an exhibitor, is calling Ms. Chou, an assistant of an exhibition center, to tell her his flight details and ask her some information about hotels.

Mr. Ryan: Hello, could I speak to Ms. Chou?

Ms. Chou: Yes, Lucy Chou speaking. What can I do for you?

Mr. Ryan: This is Ryan from Sunrise Company. I've booked a ticket to Beijing.

Ms. Chou: That's great! When will you arrive?

Mr. Ryan: I'm arriving at 11:40 a.m. tomorrow on Flight CB2415.

Ms. Chou: Do you need to **be picked up** at the airport?

Mr. Ryan: No, I'll go either by **shuttle** or by taxi. **By the way**, is it easy for me to **reserve** a room when I get there?

Ms. Chou: Yes, but it would be better to make a room reservation ahead of time. May I reserve a room for you?

Mr. Ryan: Yes, that would be better.

Ms. Chou: Well, Mr. Ryan, Beijing has a lot of excellent hotels. Let me see.

Mr. Ryan: My colleagues **recommend** three hotels—the Beijing Continental Grand Hotel, the Sun-world Hotel and the Beijing Hotel.

Ms. Chou: Well, it depends on what's important to you. All three have excellent business **facilities**. The Beijing Continental Grand Hotel is in a very quiet area and quite close to the **convention** center. It provides very good sporting facilities. The Sun-world Hotel is near the Pearl River, but it's very difficult to get a room because it often holds large **conferences** there. The restaurants boast an excellent **reputation**. The Beijing Hotel is good for relaxing. It can help arrange leisure events and so on.

Mr. Ryan: Which one would you choose?

Ms. Chou: I think I'd like to choose Beijing Continental Grand Hotel, because of the location and the **surroundings**.

Mr. Ryan: I'll follow your advice. Thanks very much for your help.

Ms. Chou: You are welcome. Please give me a phone call when you arrive in Beijing and I'll tell you where to get a taxi or shuttle bus to the hotel.

Mr. Ryan: Thank you for your help. Good-bye.

Ms. Chou: Don't mention it, Mr. Ryan. Good-bye.

Vocabulary and notes

1. pick up: to let some one get into your car, boat, *etc* and take them somewhere；接人

2. shuttle: n. the route taken or the aircraft, bus, or train used to travel frequently between two places, often relatively near each other；穿梭；穿梭班机、公共汽车等

3. by the way: used to introduce something that is not strictly part of the subject at hand；顺便说说，顺便问一下；在途中

All is not gold that glitters. 闪光的东西并不都是黄金。

4. reserve: v. to make arrangements in advance to secure a place such as a seat, ticket, table, or hotel room；预订（座位等）

5. recommend: vt. to suggest something as worthy of being accepted, used, or done；推荐；介绍；劝告；使受欢迎；托付

6. facility: n. something designed or created to provide a service or fulfill a need；设施；设备

7. convention: n. a gathering of people who have a common interest or profession；大会

8. conference: n. a meeting, sometimes lasting for several days, in which people with a common interest participate in discussions or listen to lectures to obtain information；会议；讨论；协商；联盟；（正式）讨论会；［工会、工党用语］年会

9. reputation: n. a high opinion that people hold about somebody or something；名声，名誉；声望

10. surrounding: adj. near or all around a place；周围的；附近的；n. 环境；周围的事物

Dialogue 2

Reserving a Room in a Hotel

Mr. Ryan, from a foreign trade company, calls a hotel to make a reservation, and the receptionist answers.

The **receptionist**: Hello, this is Beijing Continental Grand hotel. Is there anything I can help you?

Mr. Ryan: Yes, I'd like to **book** a room.

The receptionist: Sure, we have different types of rooms. Which would you like to choose?

Mr. Ryan: I'm not very certain. Could you give me a **brief** introduction, please?

The receptionist: Ok, our hotel provides **standard** single rooms, double rooms, and special **treatment** for VIP, accordingly.

Mr. Ryan: Thank you! I want to reserve a single room which is located between the 4th to the 7th floor. Well, I need the **room attendant** in your hotel to open the window and clean the room before I arrive there. Is that Ok?

The receptionist: Ok, sir, I have already taken some notes about your **requirements**. Now let me check. Well, one standard single room on the 6th floor and the room number is 0603; need to clean and open the window. Anything else?

Mr. Ryan: No more. Thanks! How much does it cost?

The receptionist: That is RMB 580.

Mr. Ryan: Doesn't your hotel have discount?

The receptionist: I'm terribly sorry, Sir. If you need a discount, you should be our VIP and stay here for at **least** 3 days.

Mr. Ryan: Ok, that's all right!

The receptionist: Ok. It's a great honour for us to serve you.

Mr. Ryan: Thank you very much!

Vocabulary and notes

1. receptionist: n. an employee who greets visitors, customers, or patients, answers the telephone, and makes appointments；接待员；传达员

2. book: n. a collection of printed or manuscript pages sewn or glued together along one side and bound between rigid boards or flexible covers；书籍；卷；账簿；名册；工作簿；v. to arrange for somebody to keep a place available at a specified time, e.g. at the theatre or in a restaurant；预订；登记

3. brief: adj. containing only the necessary information, without any extra details；简短的，简洁的；短暂的，草率的；n. a synopsis of a larger document or group of documents 摘要，简报；概要，诉书

4. standard: n. the level of quality or excellence attained by somebody or something；标准；水准；旗；度量衡标准

5. treatment: n. the application of medical care to cure disease, heal injuries, or ease symptoms；the usual way of dealing with a person or situation；治疗；疗法；处理；对待

6. room attendant: 客房服务员

7. requirement: n. something that is needed in order for something else to happen；要求；必要条件；必需品

8. least: adj. used to emphasize that something is so small as to be almost non-existence；最小的；最少的（little 的最高级）

Dialogue 3

Shipping Samples

Mr. Ryan wants to have his company's samples sent to a trade company in Beijing on time. Now he is having a talk with two attendants, Tom and Lucy.

Mr. Ryan: Excuse me! Where can I send a **parcel**?

Tom: At that counter over there.

Mr. Ryan: Hello. May I send a parcel to Beijing here?

Lucy: Yes. What is inside your parcel?

Mr. Ryan: Two shirts, a pair of shoes and a suit.

Lucy: By **regular** mail or air mail?

Mr. Ryan: How long does it take to go by regular mail from here to Beijing? And how long to go by air mail?

Lucy: Ah, it takes one week by regular mail while one to two days by air mail.

Mr. Ryan: How much for regular mail?

Lucy: It depends on the weight of your parcel. Let me weigh it first. It's three kilograms, so it costs 18 dollars and a **quarter** by regular mail.

Mr. Ryan: What about air mail?

Lucy: You'll have to add 20 dollars more. Which way do you prefer to?

Mr. Ryan: By air mail, please. Here is the money.

Lucy: Keep the **receipt**, please.

Mr. Ryan: **Many thanks**.

Lucy: It's my pleasure.

Vocabulary and notes

1. parcel: n. one or more things wrapped up together in paper or other packaging；包裹；小包

2. regular: adj. occurring or doing something frequently enough over a period of time to establish a pattern, though not necessarily a strict one；定期的；有规律的；合格的；整齐的；普通的

3. quarter: n. a number that is equal to one divided by four, represented by the symbol 1/4

四分之一；一刻钟

4. receipt: n. a document that you get from someone showing that you have given them money or goods；收到；收据；收入；vt. 收到

5. many thanks: 非常感谢

Dialogue 4

Receiving the Customer at the Airport

*Chen Lan (Ms. Chen), a **representative** of the foreign trade company, and her secretary, Miss Wang, are receiving their guest, Mr. Ryan.*

Mr. Ryan: Hi! I'm Ryan Smith, **sales manager** from Sunrise Company. Are you from Huaxia Company?

Ms. Chen: Yes! My name's Chen Lan, the **production manager** of Huaxia Company. Here's my **business card**. Welcome to Beijing.

Mr. Ryan: Thank you. Here's mine. Nice to meet you.

Ms. Chen: Nice to meet you, too. And this is my secretary, Miss Wang.

Miss Wang: Glad to meet you.

Mr. Ryan: Glad to meet you, too.

Ms. Chen: Have you got your **luggage**?

Mr. Ryan: Yes!

Miss Wang: Let's go this way, please. Our car is over there.

Ms. Chen: How's your **journey**?

Mr. Ryan: The flight was very good and the service on board was excellent.

Ms. Chen: Shall we go to the hotel directly? We've booked a room for you at the Beijing Continental Grand Hotel.

Mr. Ryan: Good.

Ms. Chen: Is it your first time to come to China?

Mr. Ryan: No, but my first time to Beijing.

Ms. Chen: In that case, we will make a good **arrangement** for you in Beijing. Miss Wang knows Beijing well. If you want to know something, you can ask her.

Mr. Ryan: Thank you. I am so lucky.

Ms. Chen: There's no arrangement tomorrow. Have a good rest and **recover** from the **jet lag**.

Mr. Ryan: Good idea.

Ms. Chen: The anniversary party will be hold tomorrow night. Would you like to join us?

Mr. Ryan: I'd love to. **It's my honor**.

Ms. Chen: Thank you. If you have any problems on your life or business, please don't **hesitate** to call me.

Mr. Ryan: I should thank you. You're so **thoughtful**!

Miss Wang: Here's the car. Please.

Vocabulary and notes

1. representative: n. somebody who speaks, acts, or votes on behalf of others；代表；典型；众议员；销售代表

2. sales manager: 销售经理；营业主任

3. production manager: 生产部经理

4. business card: n. a small piece of thick stiff paper that shows your name, job and the company yor work for；名片

5. luggage: n. suitcases, bags, and other items for carrying personal belongings during a journey；行李；皮箱

6. journey: n. an occasion when you travel from one place to another, especially when there is a long distance between the places；旅行；行程

7. arrangement: n. something that has to be done so that something else can happen in the future, or the making of such preparations；布置；整理；准备；安排

8. recover: v. to get back something previously lost or its equivalent；恢复；弥补；重新获得

9. jet lag: 时差感，飞行时差反应

10. it's my honor: 很荣幸

11. hesitate: vi. pause or hold back in uncertainty or unwillingness；踌躇，犹豫；不愿

12. thoughtful: adj. appearing to be deep in thought；深思的；体贴的；关切的

13. Please don't hesitate to call me. 请不要犹豫，赶紧联系我。

Activity

Make up a dialogue based on the following situation.

Suppose you are a secretary of Beijing Sunrise Foreign Trade Company. You are going to receive a VIP guest from America at the airport.

Section II *Extensive Reading*

Passage 1

The Best Way of Traveling

Whether you haven't met that special someone, or travel on business, or simply need some "alone time", traveling alone can be entirely different from going with a friend. You may fear traveling by yourself. These tips for solo travel can give you the confidence you might be looking for.

1. **Avoid** lodging with a single supplement

Some cruise lines and hotels might require two people to share the property. If you want it all to yourself, you will have to pay a single supplement so their travel provider can still make their anticipated revenue as if you brought a travel companion.

These fees will be **disclosed** before you book. If not, be sure to ask before **confirming** the reservation.

2. Stay somewhere with **multiple** positive ratings

Traveling **solo** might make you feel more **vulnerable** in an unfamiliar place. Before booking a place to stay, do a little research and only stay at a hotel or **Airbnb** property with multiple **positive** reviews. These reviews will give you a good idea of what to expect from the host, neighborhood, and if any other tenants（房客）might be sharing the property with you.

3. Meet other travelers

Another way to **break up** the **monotony** of solo travel is to meet other travelers. Your conversation doesn't have to end when you land and board the plane. In fact, two great resources can help you connect with fellow travelers and even locals. One is Couchsurfing（沙发客旅行

社交平台）(similar to Airbnb) enabling you to stay with local homeowners where you might also be able to meet other travelers.

Regardless of where you stay when you travel, you can also use Meetup to find local events and activities that are happening in town. You might be able to hang out at a certain cafe or even attend a local festival that isn't mentioned in any of the guidebooks. There are many opportunities in each city, so, be sure to check this out before you arrive.

4. Start your day early

If the idea of pub crawling（招待会）and going to nightclubs alone doesn't sound appealing, be an early bird instead. There are plenty of opportunities to go **sightseeing** alone and be completely safe if you visit a large, bustling city. Getting up early also makes it easier to avoid the crowds at popular attractions once families and those night owls leave their hotel for the day.

Summary on Traveling Alone

You might dread your next solo trip. Don't! It could really be one of the most **enjoyable** experiences you ever have. Sure, it's fun to make memories with your friends and family, but, solo travel have **plenty of** fun too. You just need to have a positive attitude. And, it wonldn't hurt you to travel alone, because technology has made the world a lot smaller than ever before.

Vocabulary and notes

1. avoid: v. to keep away from somebody or something；避免；避开；防止；回避

2. disclose: v. to reveal something that has been kept a secret；透露；泄露；揭露；使显露

3. confirm: v. to verify the truth or validity of something thought to be true or valid；确认；认可；使感觉更强烈；使确信

4. multiple: adj. a number that can be divided exactly by a particular smaller number；数量多的；多种多样的

5. solo: n. an action or feat carried out by one person alone, e.g. a flight in an aircraft or a climb up a mountain；独自；单独；独唱；独奏

6. vulnerable: adj. easily damaged by something negative or harmful；（身体上或感情上）脆弱的

7. Airbnb: 爱彼迎，一款 app，是全球民宿短租公寓预定平台

8. positive: adj. believing that good things will happen or that a situation will get better；肯定；确信；积极乐观的；自信的

9. break up: v. to divide or separate something into pieces, or interrupt its continuity；拆散；打碎；剖割（兽体等）；破坏

10. monotony: n. boredom or dullness arising from the fact that nothing different ever happens；单调乏味；千篇一律

11. regardless: adv. in spite of or ignoring setbacks, hindrances, or problems；不顾；不加理会

12. sightsee: v. to visit a place's interesting sights；观光；游览

13. summary: n. a shortened version of something that has been said or written, containing only the main points；总结；概括；概要

14. enjoyable: adj. something that is enjoyable gives you pleasure；有乐趣的；令人愉快的

15. plenty of: adj. 很多的

16. Traveling alone can be entirely different from going with a friend. 独自旅行和与朋友一起旅行完全不同。

17. If you want it all to yourself, you will have to pay a single supplement so the travel provider can still make their anticipated revenue as if you brought a travel companion. 如果你想独享这一切，你必须支付一笔额外费用，这样他们就可以像你带了一个旅伴一样赚取预期的收入。

18. These reviews will give you a good idea of what to expect from the host, neighborhood, and if any other tenants might be sharing the property with you. 这些评论会让你很好地了解房东、邻居，以及是否有其他租户会和你分享房子。

19. Regardless of where you stay when you travel, you can also use Meetup to find local events and activities that are happening in town. You might be able to hang out at a certain cafe or even attend a local festival that isn't mentioned in any of the guidebooks. 无论你旅行时住在哪里，你都可以使用 Meetup 来查找当地的活动。你也许可以在某个咖啡馆闲逛，甚至参加旅游指南中没有提到的当地节日。

20. There are plenty of opportunities to go sightseeing alone and be completely safe if you visit a large, bustling city. 如果你去一个繁华的大城市，你会有很多独自观光的机会，而且非常安全。

21. You might dread your next solo trip. Don't! It could really be one of the most enjoyable experiences you ever have. 你可能会害怕你的下一次独自旅行。千万不要害怕。这可能会是你最愉快的一次经历。

译文

　　无论你是否遇到过那个特别的人，或是出差，或者只是需要一些"独处的时间"，独自旅行与和朋友一起旅行是完全不同的。你可能害怕一个人旅行，以下几条建议或许可以让你找到自信。

　　1. 避免与另一个人合住

　　一些邮轮公司和酒店可能需要两个人合住。如果你想独享这一切，你必须支付一笔额外的费用，这样他们就可以像你带了一个旅行伙伴一样赚取预期的收入。

　　这些费用将在您预订前公布。如果没有，请务必在确认预订前询问。

　　2. 待在好评多的地方

　　独自旅行可能会让你在陌生的地方感到更脆弱。在预订住宿地之前，做一点调查，只住好评多的酒店或 Airbnb 平台上的公寓。这些评论会让你很好地了解房东、邻居，以及是否有其他租户与你分享房子。

　　3. 认识其他旅行者

　　另一种打破独自旅行所带来的单调的方法是去认识其他旅行者。你的谈话不一定非得在你着陆和登机时结束。事实上，有两个很好的资源可以帮助你与其他旅行者甚至当地人建立联系。其中一个是沙发冲浪（类似于 Airbnb）让你和当地的房主呆在一起，在那里你也可以认识其他的旅行者。

　　无论你旅行时住在哪里，你都可以使用 Meetup 来查找当地的活动。你也许可以在某个咖啡馆闲逛，甚至参加旅游指南中没有提到的当地节日。每个城市都有很多机会，所以一定要在你到达之前搜查一下。

　　4. 早点开始你的一天

　　如果独自去酒吧和去夜总会的想法听起来并不吸引人，那就做个早起的鸟儿吧。如果你去一个繁华的大都市，你会有很多独自观光的机会，而且非常安全。一旦全家人和那些夜猫子离开酒店去往景点，热门景点必然人山人海，早起可以更容易避开热门景点的人群。

　　独自旅行小结

　　你可能会害怕你的下一次独自旅行。千万不要害怕。这可能会是你最愉快的一次经历。当然，和你的朋友和家人一起旅行也是很有趣的，但是，独自旅行的人也有很多乐趣。你只需要有一个积极的态度。虽然科技使世界变得比以往任何时候都小得多，但这并没有什么坏处。

Passage 2

Beijing

Beijing, Jing for short, is the nation's political, economic, **cultural** and **educational** center as well as China's most important center for international trade and communications. **Together** with Xi'an, Luoyang（洛阳）, Kaifeng（开封）, Nanjing and Hangzhou, Beijing is one of the six ancient cities in China. It has been the heart and soul of politics and society throughout its long history and consequently there is an unparalleled wealth of **discovery** to delight and intrigue travelers as they explore Beijing's ancient past and enjoy its exciting modern development.

As the capital of the People's Republic of China, Beijing is located in northern China, close to Tianjin Municipality（直辖市）and partially surrounded by Hebei Province. The city covers an area of more than 16,410 square kilometers（6336 square miles）and has a population of 14.93 million people.

Beijing is a city with four **distinct** seasons. Its best is late spring and autumn. But autumn is taken as the golden tourist season of the year since there is, sometimes in the spring of recent years, a yellow wind. We suggest tourists visit Beijing during the months of May, September, and October when people can enjoy bright sunshine and blue skies. **An abundance of** international class **performances** are presented in May. If you like winter, you will have other chances to appreciate another **landscape** of Beijing. After skiing in Beihai and viewing the **snowy** sights on West Hill, enjoying the steaming（热气腾腾的）hotpot is the best choice, which is really the fun of tour in Beijing. Please keep warm and remember to bring your down **garments** and sweaters when you visit Beijing in the winter.

Although now Beijing is a modern and fashionable city complete with a full 21st Century vitality, you can experience authentic Beijing life and become acquainted with "old Beijing" by exploring its many teahouses, temple fairs, Beijing's Hutong（胡同）and Courtyard and enjoy the Peking Opera. You will leave with a feeling of special appreciation in your heart for this ancient city that has truly seen it all and tells its story with matchless grace, charm and vigor.

No words can adequately express all the charm of Beijing, therefore the only way to appreciate it fully is to experience it by yourself. In 2008, Beijing hosted the Olympic Games. The city had taken this opportunity to show the world something so special that everyone is sure to be awestruck by Beijing's latest accomplishments combined with its ancient history.

Vocabulary and notes

1. cultural: adj. relating to a culture or civilization；与文化有关的；文化的

2. educational: adj. relating to or concerned with education；教育的；有关教育的

3. together: adv. in company with others in a group or in a place；一起；在一起

4. discovery: n. something new that has been learned or found；发现；发觉

5. distinct: adj. clearly different and separate from others；清晰的；清楚的；明白的；明显的

6. an abundance of: 许许多多的

7. performance: n. a presentation of an artistic work such as a play or piece of music to an audience；表现；业绩；表演

8. landscape: n. an expanse of scenery of a particular type, especially as much as can be seen by the eye；景色

9. snowy: adj. characterized by the presence of snow；被雪覆盖的

10. garments: n. a piece of clothing, especially used when talking about the production and sale of clothes；服装；服饰

11. Although now Beijing is a modern and fashionable city completed with a full 21st Century vitality, you can experience authentic Beijing life and become acquainted with 'old Beijing' by exploring its many teahouses, temple fairs, Beijing's Hutong and Courtyard and enjoy the Peking Opera. 虽然现在的北京是一个充满21世纪活力的现代时尚城市，但你可以通过游览北京的众多茶馆、庙会、胡同和四合院，体验真正的北京生活，熟悉"老北京"，欣赏京剧。

译文

北京，简称京，是全国的政治、经济、文化和教育中心，也是中国最重要的国际贸易和交流中心。北京与西安、洛阳、开封、南京、杭州并称为中国六大古城。在其悠久的历史中，它一直是政治和社会的核心和灵魂，因此，游客们探索北京的过去，享受其令人兴奋的现代发展。

北京是中华人民共和国的首都，位于中国北方，靠近天津市，部分被河北省包围。这座城市的面积超过16410平方千米（6336平方英里），人口1493万。

北京是一个四季分明的城市。最好的季节是春末和秋末。但是秋天被认为是一年中的黄金旅游季节，因为这个季节秋风吹起黄叶纷飞（近年来有时候会在春天出现这一景象）。我们

建议游客在五月、九月和十月去北京旅游，那时人们可以享受明媚的阳光和蓝天。五月将有大量的国际级演出。如果你喜欢冬天，你将有其他机会欣赏北京的另一个景观。在北海滑冰、游览西山雪景后，享受热气腾腾的火锅是最好的选择，这真是北京旅游的乐趣。冬天来北京旅游时，请注意保暖，记得带羽绒服和毛衣。

虽然现在的北京是一个充满21世纪活力的现代时尚城市，但你可以通过游览北京的众多茶馆、庙会、胡同和四合院，体验真正的北京生活，熟悉"老北京"，欣赏京剧。当你离开这座古城的时候，你会对它产生一种特殊的感激之情，因为它真正见证了这一切，以无与伦比的优雅、魅力和活力讲述着它的故事。

没有语言能充分表达北京的魅力，只有亲身体验，才能充分感受北京的魅力。2008年北京将主办奥运会。北京将借此机会向世界展示它的特别之处，让每个人都对北京最新的成就和古老的历史感到敬畏。

Section III *Case Analysis in Intercultural Communication*

Same Language, Different Behavior

An American traveled to England and stayed with a friend. During his stay, the American decided to talk to the Englishman about something that was bothering him.

American: I feel uncomfortable with many of the people here, but I'm not sure why. I speak the same language, so there shouldn't be any problem. Back home, I usually get along with people. You know that I'm very friendly.

Englishman: Yes, that's true, but you're friendly in the way that Americans are.

American: I'm not sure I understand.

Englishman: Well, for example, at the meeting the other night, you immediately called people by their first names. We do that here but not for the first meeting.

American: That's how we make people feel comfortable. People feel friendlier toward each other when they use first names.

Englishman: It's different here. For example, when you met my boss you should have used his last name. Besides, there's something else that you do that English people don't often do.

American: What's that?

Englishman: You touch people on the shoulder quite a bit, especially when you compliment them.

American: I guess I've never thought about that before. I suppose that is what I do at home.

（Deena R. levine et al.,1987）

分析：这对美国人来说是一个文化冲击，尽管他们在与英国人交流时可能仍然存在同样的语言问题。他不会停下来想，他可能要做不同的事情。幸运的是，有人能帮助他理解并迅速学会在英国他需要做的不仅仅是说英语。

Section IV Practical Writing: Fax

传真是将文字、图表、照片等记录在纸面上的静止图像，通过扫描和光电变换，变成电信号，经各类信道传送到目的地，在接收端通过一系列逆变换过程，获得与发送原稿相似记录副本的通信方式。

传真既有信函的特征又有备忘录、电子邮件等的特点。酒店预定表格的传真一般包括以下几个部分：收件人地址、寄件人姓名、入住时间、预定房间的数量和类型、付款方式、寄件人电话号码、传真号码和电子邮箱地址。

Sample

To: XX Company

From: Mr. Wang

Date: 2000/1/23

Fax No: 2233666

Subject: Providing Information

Content:

Dear Mr. Smith,

It was a pleasure to meet you last week and learned that you were interested in our promotion program. We are sending you details of our March promotion plan. Because the time is urgent and the deadline has passed, we hope you can confirm it as soon as possible. Thank you for your for your kind intention and I look forward to your prompt reply.

Best regards.

Practice

假设你叫 Ryan Smith，于 2020 年 11 月 12 日将赴北京参加外贸交易会，拟在那里停留 10 天。请给接洽的北京东方贸易有限公司处发一个传真，说明你们到达的时间，要求帮忙订两个单人间，你们的付款方式为信用卡。传真号码：0086-778-2287235。

Practice

To:

From:

Date:

Fax No.:

Subject:

Content:

Dear Sirs,

Section V *Grammar: Adjective & Adverb*（形容词及副词）

一、形容词

1. 作定语

例：It's a beautiful day today.

注意：形容词修饰 something, anything, nothing 等复合不定代词时要后置。

例：I have something important to tell you.

以 a- 开头的表状态的形容词（afraid, alone, awake, asleep, alive, alike, ashamed, unable, worth）要后置。

例：He was the only man awake at that time.

2. 作表语

例：Don't feel sad. Tasting good, this kind of cake sells well.

3. 作宾补

例：We must keep our classroom clean.

4. 作状语

例：The boy went to school, cold and hungry.

5. 以 ly 结尾的形容词

如：friendly, lovely, lively, silly, fatherly, motherly, weekly, daily, monthly, yearly, deadly, lonely, manly, timely, likely。

6. 表倍数的几种句式

（1）……倍数 +as+ 形容词原级 +as……

（2）……倍数 + 比较级 +than ……

（3）……倍数 +the+ 名词（size/length / width / height /depth）+ of ……

（4）The + 名词 + be + ……倍数 + what 从句

（5）The + 名词 + be + ……倍数 + that/ those of ……

例：Asia is four times as large as Europe.= Asia is four times larger than Europe.= Asia is four times the size of Europe.

例：The output of this year is 3 times that of 2008.

例：The output of this year is 3 times what it was in 2008.

7. 形容词加 ly 变副词的规则

（1）一般情况加 ly，如：quick—quickly, brave—bravely, immediate—immediately。

（2）以 "y" 结尾的，且读音为 / i /，先将 "y" 改成 "i"，再加 "ly"，如：happy—happily, heavy—heavily, angry—angrily, busy—busily, easy—easily。但是如果读音为 /ai/，直接加 ly，如：dry—dryly, shy—shyly。

（3）le 结尾，去 e 加 y，如：y: simple—simply, gentle—gently, comfortable—comfortably, possible—possibly, probable—probably, terrible—terribly, considerable—considerably, incredible—incredibly。但是 whole—wholly 例外。

（4）元音字母加 e 结尾，去 e 加 ly，如：true—truly, due—duly。绝大多数辅音字母加 e 结尾的形容词直接加 ly，如：polite-politely, wide—widely, wise—wisely, nice—nicely。

（5）ll 结尾只加 y，如：full—fully, dull—dully。

（6）ic 结尾加 ally，如：basic—basically, scientific—scientifically。但是 public—publicly 例外。

8. 形容词的比较级及最高级变化规则

（1）一般加 -er 或 the -est。如：strong—stronger—the strongest

（2）以字母 e 结尾直接加 r 或 st。如：late—later—latest, fine—finer—finest, nice—

nicer—nicest, wide—wider—widest。

（3）需双写结尾字母后再加 er 或 est。如：glad—gladder—gladdest, hot—hotter—hottest, thin—thinner—thinnest, big—bigger—biggest, fat—fatter—fattest, wet—wetter—wettest, sad—sadder—saddest, red—redder—reddest, slim—slimmer—slimmest。

（4）变 y 为 i 再加 -er 或 -est。如：angry—angrier—angriest, merry—merrier—merriest, pretty—prettier—prettiest, ugly—uglier—ugliest, early—earlier—earliest, easy—easier—easiest, happy—happier—happiest。

（5）其他双音节或多音节词，加 more 或 most。如：enthusiastic—more enthusiastic—most enthusiastic。

9. 不规则变化

good / well—better—most, bad/ ill—worse—worst, little—less—least, much/ many—more—most, far—farther 距离更远 /further 距离更远或程度更深入 —farthest/furthest; old—older（指年龄较长的；新旧）/ elder（只指年龄较长的）—oldest/ eldest。

二、副词

1. 作状语

例：Look at the photo carefully.

2. 少数地点或时间副词

如：here、there、home、abroad、upstairs、above、below、yesterday、today、tomorrow 等作后置定语。

例：The people there were very friendly. Do you know the man upstairs?

3. 作表语

如：in、out、on、back、up、down、off、away、downstairs、upstairs 等。

例：Is the radio on or off?

4. 作宾补

例：Sorry to have kept you up so late.

5. 词性相同、词意不同的副词

deep 深地（具体的深度）—deeply 深深地（抽象概念）；

close（靠近地）—closely（密切地）；

high（高地）—highly（高度地）；

wide（宽地）—widely（广泛地）；

late（晚）—lately（最近）；

free（免费）—freely（自由地）

hard（努力地、辛苦地）—hardly（几乎不）；

most（最，很）—mostly（主要地），几乎全部；

near（靠近）—nearly（几乎，差不多）。

例：You have come too late. What have you been doing lately.

例：You can eat free in my restaurant whenever you like. You may speak freely, say what you like.

例：You have to work hard. What he said was hardly true.

例：Which part of the concert did you like most. It is a most interesting film. She is mostly out on Sundays.

6. 副词固定搭配

如：wide open（敞开，睁得很大）；wide awake（完全没睡着）；deep into the night（到深夜）；deep in thought（深思）；here and there（到处）；up and down（上上下下）。

三、常用句型

1. 比较级 +and+ 比较级（越来越……）。

例：My hometown is becoming more and more beautiful.

2. the+ 比较级，the+ 比较级（越……，越……）。

例：The older I get, the happier I feel.

3. "比较级 +than + any other+ 单数名词"可替换最高级。

例：Tom runs faster than any other student in his class. = Tom runs the fastest in his class.

4. "比较级 +than + all the other+ 复数名词"可替换最高级。

例：She is more beautiful than all the other girls in our school. = She is the most beautiful girl in our school.

5. "否定词 + 比较级 +than + 其他"替换最高级。

例：Nothing is more valuable than health for us. = Health is the most valuable for us.

6. "否定词 +as/so + 原级 +as"替换最高级。

例：No student is as / so diligent as Jim in our class. = Jim is the most diligent student in our class.

7. the + 形容词比较级 + of……（两者中较……的一个）。

例：He is the taller of the two brothers.

8. one of 形容词最高级 + 名词 + 表示范围的状语。

例：Shanghai is one of the biggest cities in our country.

9. 序数词 + 形容词最高级 + 名词。

例：Africa is the second largest continent in the world.

10. 倍数 +as + 形容词 / 副词 +as；倍数 + 形容词 / 副词的比较级 +than；倍数 +the+ 名词 (height/length/depth/size) of；倍数 +what 从句。

例：Asia is four times as large as Europe.

11. The + 名词 +be+ 倍数 +that/those of。

例：The production now is three times what it was ten years ago.

Exercise 1：Adjective（形容词）

一、单项选择

1. I don't think the movie is _____.
　A. interesting　　B. interested　　C. interest　　D. interests

2. We were very _____ to see each other again in this bookstore.
　A. pleased　　B. surprising　　C. happily　　D. angrily

3. Lily is very _____ the news.
　A. surprise in　　B. surprise with　　C. surprised at　　D. surprised for

4. —How does Kelly like her new school?
　—She _____ with the environment.
　A. can't satisfy　　B. isn't satisfied　　C. doesn't satisfy　　D. hasn't satisfied

5. The doctor was not _____ when he heard the _____ words.
　A. frightening; frightening　　B. frightened; frightened
　C. frightening; frightened　　D. frightened; frightening

6. I am afraid that I can't go to the party, because I don't feel very _____.
　A. terribly　　B. well　　C. good　　D. badly

7. Looking _____ at his father, the little boy looked _____.
　A. happy; good　　B. happy; well　　C. sadly; sad　　D. sad; sadly

8. I don't feel _____ today. I'd better have a rest.

A. good B. well C. nice D. health

9. In hot summer eggs will without doubt go _____ easily.

A. terribly B. terrible C. badly D. bad

10. Lucy does morning exercises every day, so she looks very _____.

A. tired B. good C. well D. happy

11. The _____ girl was taken to the nearest hospital and received treatment.

A. ill B. sick C. good D. clever

12. We are _____ of the part-time work.

A. ill B. sick C. full D. filled

13. She has not been at school, because she is _____.

A. ill B. well C. fine D. nice

14. I have worked for ten hours without rest, so I am feeling tired and _____.

A. asleep B. sleepy C. sleeping D. sleep

15. They have never seen _____ interesting play.

A. such B. such an C. so D. such a

16. This is _____ book _____ I'd like to read once more.

A. such an interesting; that
B. so interesting; that
C. such an interesting; as
D. a so interesting; as

17. They are excited because they haven't seen _____ movie.

A. so wonderful
B. a so wonderful
C. such wonderful
D. such a wonderful

18. Lily was sick yesterday, but she is _____ to go to school today.

A. enough good
B. good enough
C. enough well
D. well enough

19. The dress was so _____ that she decided to buy it.

A. much B. little C. expensive D. cheap

20. The room is _____ larger than theirs.

A. more B. quite C. very D. much

二、用所给词的适当形式填空

1. This box is _____ (heavy) than that one.

2. I think this film is not so _____ (interest) as that one.

3. Mike is _____ (tall) than his brother.

4. I think ability is _____ (important) than appearance.

5. This bag is _____ (expensive) than that one.

三、翻译

1. 迈克是班上最高的。

2. 这条裙子是三条裙子中最贵的。

3. 黄河是中国第二长河。

4. 在我们学校，语文老师最忙。

5. 他比我大三岁。

Exercise 2：Adverb（副词）

一、单项选择

1. —It's reported that Fuxa high-speed train can go as ____ as 420 km an hour.
   —Wow, how amazing!

   A. fast　　　　B. faster　　　　C. fastest　　　　D. the fastest

2. —Did Kelly do her best in the final exam?
   —No, but of all the students she did ____.

   A. the most careful　　　　B. more careful
   C. most carefully　　　　D. more carefully

3. —Confucius Institute（孔子学院）has been set up in many other countries.
   —Yes, Chinese is ____ spoken in those countries. I am proud of that as a Chinese.

   A. hardly　　　B. widely　　　C. never　　　D. seldom

4. —Mike，have you got any plans for winter holiday?
   —Not yet.____I'll go back to Amoy with my friends.

   A. Maybe　　　B. Actually　　　C. Generally　　　D. Perhaps

5. ____ is your father? Is he fine?

   A. What　　　B. How　　　C. Where　　　D. When

6. Drivers should drive____ when they are passing by a school.

   A. fast　　　B. quickly　　　C. slowly　　　D. freely

7. It rained ____ yesterday.

A. heavily   B. quietly   C. hardly   D. quickly

8. The CET6 is very important. We must treat it ____.

A. serious   B. seriously   C. careless   D. carelessly

9. I can't hear the lecturer ____ with so much noise outside.

A. clearly   B. slowly   C. warmly   D. bravely

10. You should think ____ before making the final decision.

A. quickly   B. seriously   C. proudly   D. slowly

11. Kate felt so tired last night that she ____ fell asleep in bed after lying down.

A. immediately   B. suddenly   C. frequently   D. recently

12. Bill spoke so ____ that I could hardly hear him.

A. loudly   B. quietly   C. clearly   D. patiently

13. Lily doesn't like staying at home. She ____ goes traveling in summer holidays.

A. never   B. seldom   C. always   D. often

14. —____ will you fly to Hongkong?
    —In two days.

A. How long   B. How often   C. How soon   D. How far

15. —____ do you go to the library, Kate?
    —Every week.

A. How long   B. How often   C. How soon   D. How far

16. —My sister Linda always thinks ____ anyone else.
    —Oh, she is a thoughtful girl.

A. more carefully than   B. more careful than

C. less carefully than   D. less careful than

17. —Do you think Kate sings as ____ as Lucy in the show I Am a Singer?
    —No, I don t think so. I think Kate sings ____ .

A. good; better   B. better; well

C. well; better   D. good; well

18. It is a world of flowers in spring in Zhangzhou. You can see flowers ____.

A. there   B. here

C. somewhere   D. everywhere

19. Skimming is a kind of reading strategy. It means reading an article ____ to find the

main idea without reading every word.

A. quickly　　　　B. carefully　　　　C. slowly　　　　D. clearly

20. "Left-behind" children ____ see their parents, because their parents work in big cities, leaving them behind in the countryside to be with their grandparents.

A. always　　　　B. hardly　　　　C. often　　　　D. ever

Unit 3

Promoting the Products

扫一扫查看
本章教学PPT

Learning Objectives

【About Knowledge】

1. To describe the products.
2. To promote the products.
3. To get to know more about tea expositions.
4. To know more about the verb.

【About Skills】

To know more about writing the letter of thanks.

Section 1 *Dialogues*

Dialogue 1

Promoting the Silk Blouse at the Booth

Mr. Ryan, an exhibitor, is talking with Ms. Ding, a saleswoman in a booth.

Mr. Ryan: I saw your **exhibits** yesterday. I found some of them are **fine in quality and beautiful in design**. The exhibition has successfully **displayed** to me what your corporation handles. I've gone over the catalogue and the **pamphlets** enclosed in your last letter. I have got some idea of your **exports**. I'm interested in your silk **blouse**.

Ms. Ding: Our silks are known for good quality. They are one of our traditional exports.

Silk blouses are brightly coloured and beautifully **designed**. They enjoy great popularity **overseas** and are always in great demand.

Mr. Ryan: Some of them are of the latest styles. I have a feeling that we can do a lot of trade in this line. We wish to establish business **relations** with you.

Ms. Ding: So do we.

Mr. Ryan: Concerning our financial position, credit standing and trade reputation, you may refer to our bank, or to our local chamber of commerce or inquiry agencies.

Ms. Ding: Thank you for your information. As you know, our **corporation** is a state-operated one. We always trade with foreign countries on the basis of equality and mutual **benefit**. Establishing business relations between us will be to our mutual benefit. I have no doubt that it will **bring about** benefit between us.

Mr. Ryan: That sounds interesting. I'll send a fax home. As soon as I receive the definite answer, I'll give you a specific answer.

Ms. Ding: We'll then make an offer as soon as possible. I hope a lot of business will be put through between us.

Mr. Ryan: So do I.

Ms. Ding: I hope everything would be smooth.

Mr. Ryan: That's what I want to say.

Ms. Ding: I'll give you the lowest price in the future.

Mr. Ryan: Thank you.

Vocabulary and notes

1. exhibit: n. something shown to the public；展览品；证据；展示会

2. fine in quality and beautiful in design: 品质优良，设计美观

3. display: v. to show, make visible or apparent；显示；表现

4. pamphlet: n. a small book usually having a cover；小册子；活页文选

5. export: n. to send goods for sale or exchange to other countries；出口；出口商品；输出额

6. blouse: n. a tunic, sometimes loose and sometimes very snug, that is a part of some military uniforms；a woman's loose-fitting shirt；（女式）短上衣

7. design: n. a drawing or other graphical representation of something that shows how it is

to function or be made；设计；设计方案；构思；安排

8. overseas: adv. across or beyond a sea, especially in another country；在国外；向海外

9. relation: n. a meaningful connection or association between two or more things, e.g. one based on the similarity or relevance of one thing to another；关联；联系；亲戚；亲属

10. corporation: n. a company recognized by law as a single body with its own powers and liabilities, separate from those of the individual members；法人；（大）公司

11. benefit: n. something that has a good effect or promotes well-being；益处；优势；成效

12. bring about: to make something happen；造成；带来

Dialogue 2

Promoting the Leather Products at the Booth

Mr. David, from a foreign trade company, is talking about products with Ms. Li at a booth showing leather bags.

Mr. David: Hello, Ms. Li.

Ms. Li: Hello, Mr. David, glad to see you again.

Mr. David: I'm very interested in your products, and would like to talk something about that. Your products seem quite new to us.

Ms. Li: I'm glad to hear that. My **firm** has wide business relations with many corporations in your country. Every year, we export a lot of our products to **European** countries.

Mr. David: Well, we worked on **leather** products only for two years, but we are in a position to place large orders with **competitive** suppliers.

Ms. Li: That's fine. Our leather bags have enjoyed a high reputation in the European market. Have you got anything in mind that you're interested in?

Mr. David: Well, I find article No.338 is rather attractive.

Ms. Li: It's our newest designed one. **Compared** with the old ones, it is much better in style. Reports from different markets show that this model is the choice of discriminating buyers.

Mr. David: You know, Ms. Li, quality is as much important as the price.

Ms. Li: Yes. This style is an **improvement** upon the old styles in many aspects. We pay much attention not only to its quality but also to its cost. After studying our samples and price list, I'm sure you will be **satisfied**.

Mr. David: Do you have any discount? If the price is reasonable, we will place an order of a large quantity.

Ms. Li: I'm sorry. Mr. David. This is our rock **bottom** price. When I fixed the price with you last time. I mentioned that it was for **the trial order** only, just to help you to get a start. That's an exceptional case. We can't close any more business on the same basis, to say nothing of making reductions. If you find it unworkable, we have no other choice but to **call the deal off**.

Vocabulary and notes

1. firm: n. a group of people who form a commercial organization selling goods or services；公司；企业；事务所；商行

2. European: adj. relating to Europe or its peoples, languages, or cultures；欧洲的；全欧的；欧盟的

3. leather: n. the processed hide of animals with the fur or feathers removed；皮革；皮外套

4. competitive: adj. involving or decided by competition；竞争的；（比……）更好的；有竞争力的

5. compare: v. to examine two or more people or things in order to discover similarities and differences between them；比较；对比；与……类似（或相似）

6. improvement: n. the process of making something better or of becoming better；改进；改善；改进处；改善的事物

7. satisfied: adj. pleased with what has happened or with what you have achieved；满意的；满足的；欣慰的；确信的

8. bottom: n. the lowest or deepest part of something；底部；水底；底面；臀部

9. the trial order: 试订货

10. call the deal off: 取消交易

Dialogue 3

Negotiating about Detailed Information of the Products

Mr. Carl is talking about the product specifications, product life and after-sales problems with Mr. Chou.

Mr. Carl: This is the model I am interested in.

Mr. Chou: I should be very happy to give you any **further information** you need.

Mr. Carl: Yes. What are the **specifications**?

Mr. Chou: If you refer to the **brochure**, you'll find all the specifications there.

Mr. Carl: Ah, yes. Now what about service life?

Mr. Chou: Our tests **indicate** that this model has a service life of at least four years.

Mr. Carl: Is that an average figure for this type of **equipment**?

Mr. Chou: Oh no, far from it. That's about one year longer than any other **makes** in its price range.

Mr. Carl: Now what happens if something goes wrong when we're using it.

Mr. Chou: If that were to happen, please **contact our nearest agent** and he'll send someone round immediately.

Vocabulary and notes

1. further information: 更多信息；进一步的信息；

2. specification: n. a detailed description, especially one providing information needed to make, build, or produce something；规范；规格；明细单；说明书

3. brochure: n. a booklet or pamphlet that contains descriptive information or advertising；资料（或广告）手册

4. indicate: v. to be or provide a sign, signal, or symptom that something exists or is true；指示；表明；显示；指出

5. equipment: n. the tools, clothing, or other items needed for a particular activity or purpose；设备；装备；器材；配备

6. make: n. the name or type of a machine, piece of equipment, *etc.* that is made by a particular company；品牌，牌子

7. contact our nearest agent: 联系我们最近的办事处

Dialogue 4

Receiving the Customer

Mr. Peter is talking about the colored pen series with Ms. Wang.

Ms. Wang: Good morning, welcome to our company.

Mr. Peter: Good morning. I'm Peter, ABC company's sales manager. I want to know some information of your company's products.

Ms. Wang: Ok, our company **is specialized in** the processing and sales of different kinds of pens. Now, we put six kinds of our company's products on the booth. In general, our products are beautiful and **decent**, **cheap and fine**. It's **suitable** for all kinds of people.

Mr. Peter: Can you introduce the **latest** product?

Ms. Wang: Ok. Our latest product is the colored pen series. It has 12 kinds of color, such as gold yellow, red, pink, purple, black and so on. Today we take the gold yellow one. This series of colored pen features its variety in color, which can be more closely to meet people's needs. In addition, it uses **high-end** technology to **solve** the problem of **dripping**, and it's very cheap and **durable**. It only costs you 2 yuan to own one piece of it.

Mr. Peter: Can you give us some discount?

Ms. Wang: Of course. Our company deals in **wholesale sale**. The wholesale price is 1.5 yuan. As you are our regular customer, we can get it at the price of 1.4 yuan.

Mr. Peter: Well, we need further discussion.

Ms. Wang: Sure, we are ready for a further discussion with you in the conference room. This way, please.

Mr. Peter: Okay.

Vocabulary and notes

1. be specialized in: 专门从事；专攻；以……为专业

2. decent: adj. conforming to accepted standards of moral behavior；像样的；相当不错的；尚好的；正派的

3. cheap and fine: 价廉物美；物美价廉

4. suitable: adj. of the right type or quality for a particular purpose or occasion；合适的；

适宜的；适当的；适用的

5. latest: adj. most recent, or newest；最新的；最近的；最后的

6. high-end: adj. expensive and likely to appeal to sophisticated and discerning people；高档的；高端的；价高质优的

7. solve: v.to find a way of dealing successfully with a problem or difficulty；解决；处理；解答；破解

8. drip: v. to fall as drops of liquid, or let liquid fall as drops；（液体）滴下

9. durable: adj. able to stay in good condition for a long time and after being used a lot；耐用的；耐久的；长期的；长久的

10. wholesale sale: 批发销售

Activity

Make up a dialogue based on the following situation.

Suppose you are a salesman from Beijing Sunrise Foreign Trade Company, you're going to promote your products, a new type of cellphone, to your customer from America.

The features of the new type of cellphone are as follows:

Fashionable designs;

Advanced Android system;

A wealth of application programs you can choose;

More clear show of movies and 3D games;

Big screen for 5.7 inches, etc.

Section II Extensive Reading

Passage 1

The Tea Exposition Cross Straits

The Seventh Tea **Exposition** Cross Straits（海峡两岸）will be held in Wuyishan（武夷山）which is famous for tea and **is honored as** "World Cultural and Natural **Heritage**" on November 16-18, 2013. The Tea Exposition is hosted by General Office of the Fujian **Provincial** People's Government, National Department of Agriculture, and the Association for Relations across the Taiwan

Straits and so on and **undertook** by the People's Government of Nanping.

It **mainly sets up** two exhibition（展览会）halls that **involve** a total of 1200 standard exhibition positions. Taiwan exhibition area is so **conspicuous** that people **are apt to** communicate with visitors. The **theme** of tea exposition is "Tea and Health". The tea exposition mainly **showcased** the latest products and **achievements** of the **cross-straits** and the overseas in tea, tea set, tea cake, tea ceremony and other fields.

In particular, it is also combined（联合）with the Tea Cultural Festival and opened a series of special activities, such as the welcome **banquet**, cross-straits gala and cross-strait tea king game, I believe these activities would be loved and welcomed by the **compatriots** across the straits and the overseas（海外）. According to the characteristic of tea exposition, the newspaper will always pay attention to the development and dynamic of tea exposition, interview people optionally to understand their feelings and opinions of tea exposition as well as present the influence of The Seventh Tea Exposition between Cross-Straits in Wuyishan.

（来源：www. the exposition. com）

Vocabulary and notes

1. exposition: n. a large exhibition, in which something such as goods art are shown to the public；（产品的）展销；商品交易会

2. be honored as: 被尊为；被誉为

3. heritage: n. a country's or area's history and historical buildings and sites that are considered to be of interest and value to present generations；遗产

4. provincial: adj. belonging to or coming from a province 省的；一级行政区的

5. undertake: v. to agree to be responsible for a job or a project and do it；承担；从事；负责；承诺

6. mainly: adv. to a large extent or in most cases；大多；大部分；主要地

7. set up: 建立；创立

8. involve: v. to contain or include something as a necessary element；需要；包含；牵涉

9. conspicuous: adj. easily or clearly visible；易见的；明显的；惹人注意的

10. be apt to: 倾向于；有……倾向的

11. theme: n. the subject of a discourse, discussion, piece of writing, or artistic composition；主题；主旋律

A small leak will sink a great ship. 一个小漏洞可能弄沉一艘大轮船。

12. showcase: v. to present something or somebody in a way that is designed to attract attention and admiration；展示

13. achievement: n. something that somebody has succeeded in doing, usually with effort；成就；成绩

14. cross-straits: 海峡两岸的

15. banquet: n. an elaborate formal meal attended by many guests, often held in honor of a particular person or occasion and followed by speeches；宴会

16. compatriot: n. somebody from the same country as another person；同胞；同国人

17. The Tea Exposition is hosted by General Office of the Fujian Provincial People's Government, National Department of Agriculture, and the Association for Relations across the Taiwan Straits and so on and undertook by the People's Government of Nanping. 茶博会由福建省人民政府办公厅、国家农业部、海峡两岸关系协会等主办，南平市人民政府承办。

18. It mainly sets up two exhibition halls that involve a total of 1200 standard exhibition positions, Taiwan exhibition area is so conspicuous that people are apt to communicate with visitors. 该茶博会主要设置两个展厅，共 1200 个标准展位，台湾展区十分醒目，易于与游客交流。

19. The theme of tea exposition is "Tea and Health". 此次茶博会的主题是"茶与健康"。

20. I believe these activities would be loved and welcomed by the compatriots across the Straits and the overseas. 相信这些活动一定会受到海峡两岸同胞和海外同胞的喜爱和欢迎。

 译文

第七届海峡两岸茶博会

第七届海峡两岸茶博会将于 2013 年 11 月 16 日至 18 日在以茶著称、被誉为"世界文化和自然遗产"的武夷山举行。茶博会由福建省人民政府办公厅、国家农业部、海峡两岸关系协会等主办，南平市人民政府承办。

该茶博会主要设置两个展厅，共 1200 个标准展位，台湾展区十分醒目，易于与游客交流。此次茶博会的主题是"茶与健康"，主要展示了两岸与海外在茶叶、茶具、茶饼、茶道等领域的最新产品和成果。

特别的是，此次茶博会还结合茶文化节，开展了一系列活动，如欢迎宴会、两岸联欢晚会、两岸茶王赛等，相信这些活动一定会受到海峡两岸同胞和海外同胞的喜爱和欢迎。根据

茶博会的特色，报社将始终关注茶博会的发展动态，有选择地采访人们，了解他们对茶博会的感受和看法，同时介绍第七届两岸茶博会对武夷山的影响。

Passage 2

On the Belt and Road Initiative

The Belt and Road Initiative is a way for **win-win cooperation** that promotes development and prosperity and a road towards peace and friendship by **enhancing** mutual understanding and **trust**, and **strengthening** all-round exchanges（交流）. The Chinese government advocates peace and cooperation, openness and inclusiveness, mutual learning and mutual benefit. It **promotes** practical cooperation（合作）in all fields, and works to build a community of shared interests, destiny and responsibility（责任）featuring mutual political trust, economic **integration** and cultural inclusiveness. The Belt and Road run through the continents of Asia, **Europe** and Africa, connecting the **vibrant** East Asia economic circle at one end and developed European economic circle at the other, and passing countries with huge potential for economic（经济的）development.

The Silk Road Economic Belt focuses on bringing together China, Central Asia, Russia and Europe (the Baltic), linking China with the Persian Gulf and the Mediterranean Sea through Central Asia and West Asia, and connecting China with Southeast Asia, South Asia and the Indian Ocean. The 21st-Century Maritime Silk Road is designed to go from China's coast to Europe through the South China Sea and the Indian Ocean in one route, and from China's coast through the South China Sea to the South Pacific（太平洋）in the other.

On land, the Initiative will focus on jointly building a new Eurasian Land Bridge and developing China-Mongolia-Russia, China-Central Asia-West Asia and China-Indochina Peninsula（半岛）economic corridors by taking advantage of international transport routes, relying on core cities along the Belt and Road and using key economic industrial parks as cooperation platforms. At sea, the Initiative will focus on jointly building smooth, secure and efficient transport routes connecting major sea ports along the Belt and Road. The China-Pakistan Economic Corridor and the Bangladesh-China-India-Myanmar Economic Corridor（长廊）are closely related to the Belt and Road Initiative, and **therefore** require closer cooperation and greater progress. The Initiative is an ambitious economic vision of the opening-up of and cooperation among the countries along the Belt and Road. Countries should work in concert and move towards the objectives of mutual（相互的）benefit and security. To be specific, they need to improve the region's **infrastructure**, and put in place a secure and efficient network of land, sea and air passages, lifting their connectivity to a higher level; further enhance trade and investment facilitation, establish a network of free trade areas that meet high standards, **maintain** closer economic ties, and deepen political trust; enhance cultural exchanges; encourage different civilizations to learn from each other and flourish（繁荣）together; and promote mutual understanding, peace and friendship among people of all countries.

Vocabulary and notes

1. The Belt and Road Initiative: 一带一路倡议

2. win-win: adj. describes a situation in which all parties benefit in some way；对各方都有益的；双赢的

3. cooperation: n. a situation in which people or organizations work together to achieve a result that will benefit all of them；合作；配合

4. enhance: v. to improve or add to the strength, worth, beauty, or other desirable quality of something；提高；增强；增进

5. trust: n. something entrusted to somebody to be responsible for；信任；信托；相信；信赖

6. strengthen: v. to make something stronger or more powerful, or increase in strength or power；加强；增强；巩固

7. promote: v. to raise somebody to a more senior job or a higher position or rank；促进；提升；振兴；宣传

8. integration: n. the process of combining with other things in a single larger unit or system；一体化；结合；融入群体或社会

9. Europe: n. the second smallest continent after Australia, lying west of Asia, north of Africa, and east of the Atlantic Ocean；欧洲；欧盟

10. vibrant: adj. seeming to quiver or pulsate with energy or activity；充满生机的；生气勃勃的

11. therefore: adv. as a result of the reason that has just been mentioned；因此

12. infrastructure: n. the most basic level of organizational structure in a complex body or system that serves as a foundation for the rest；（国家或机构的）基础设施

13. maintain: v. to make sure that something stays at the same level, rate, or standard；维

护；保持；坚持；抚养

14. The Belt and Road Initiative is a way for win-win cooperation that promotes development and prosperity and a road towards peace and friendship by enhancing mutual understanding and trust, and strengthening all-round exchanges. "一带一路"倡议是促进发展与繁荣的合作共赢的方式，是通过增进相互了解和信任，加强全方位交流而通往和平与友谊的道路。

15. The 21st-Century Maritime Silk Road is designed to go from China's coast to Europe through the South China Sea and the Indian Ocean in one route, and from China's coast through the South China Sea to the South Pacific in the other. 21世纪海上丝绸之路分为两条线路，一条从中国沿海到欧洲，途经中国南海和印度洋，另一条则从中国沿海经过中国南海到达南太平洋。

16. At sea, the Initiative will focus on jointly building smooth, secure and efficient transport routes connecting major sea ports along the Belt and Road. The China-Pakistan Economic Corridor and the Bangladesh-China-India-Myanmar Economic Corridor are closely related to the Belt and Road Initiative, and therefore require closer cooperation and greater progress. 海上丝绸之路则致力于共同建设连接"一带一路"沿线主要海港的畅通、安全、高效的运输通道。中国—巴基斯坦经济走廊和孟加拉国—中国—印度—缅甸经济走廊与"一带一路"倡议密切相关，因此需要更紧密的合作和更大的进步。

译文

论"一带一路"倡议

"一带一路"倡议是促进发展与繁荣的合作共赢的方式，是通过增进相互了解信任，加强全方位交流而通往和平与友谊的道路。中国政府主张和平合作、开放包容、相互学习、互利共赢，推动各领域务实合作，努力构建政治互信、经济融合、文化包容的利益共同体、命运共同体、责任共同体。"一带一路"贯穿亚洲、欧洲和非洲大陆，一端连接着充满活力的东亚经济圈，另一端则连着发达的欧洲经济圈，穿过了具有巨大经济发展潜力的国家。

丝绸之路经济带致力于将中国、中亚、俄罗斯和欧洲（波罗的海）连接起来；通过中亚和西亚连接中国与波斯湾和地中海；将中国与东南亚、南亚和印度洋连接起来。21世纪上海丝绸之路分为两条线路，一条从中国沿海到欧洲，途经中国南海和印度洋，另一条则从中国沿海经过中国南海到达南太平洋。

陆上丝绸之路将以共建新亚欧大陆桥为重点，利用国际运输通道，发展中国—蒙古—俄罗斯、中国—中亚—西亚和中印半岛经济走廊，依托"一带一路"沿线核心城市，以重点经济产业园区为合作平台。海上丝绸之路则致力于共同建设连接"一带一路"沿线主要海港的畅通、安全、高效的运输通道。中国—巴基斯坦经济走廊和孟加拉国—中国—印度—缅甸经济走廊与"一带一路"倡议密切相关，因此需要更密切的合作和更大的进展。该倡议是"一带一路"沿线国家开放合作的宏伟经济愿景。各国应齐心协力，朝着互利和安全的目标迈进。具体来说，要完善地区基础设施，建立安全高效的陆海空通道网络，提高互联互通水平；进一步加强贸易和投资便利化，建立高标准的自由贸易区网络，密切经济联系，深化政治互信，加强文化交流，鼓励不同文明相互借鉴、共同繁荣，促进各国人民相互了解、和平友好。

Section III Case Analysis in Intercultural Communication

Hospitality

Lin had traveled 20 hours from Beijing to New York. He needed a good meal. His American friend, Mike, met him. But Mike only offered him a plate of roasted chicken and a glass of orange juice. Lin was used to having a main course, and asked Mike if he had any rice. Mike said he only had fried noodles, and Lin had to **make do with**（设法应付）it.

Though Lin knew Americans didn't care very much about what food they ate, he still felt surprised because he had taken Mike to the most famous duck restaurant in Beijing—Quanjude—when he arrived in Beijing.

Question for discussion

Why did Lin feel surprised? Offer some advices to him about adjusting to his new environment in America.

分析：

（1）在好客的话题上，中国人强调热情和展现彼此友谊。他们带客人去一家著名或豪华的餐厅吃一顿非常好（昂贵）的饭菜，以示他们的好客。并且中国人习惯于吃大餐。他们摆放的菜越多，便越能表现出热情和友爱。

（2）在西方国家，人们强调自由。他们给客人很大的自由选择自己的食物。西方人往往只有一个主菜和一些果汁或甜点，在中国人看来这样对待客人太随意了。

（3）林现在处于美国文化当中，他应该先了解美国的待客习俗，尽快适应新生活方式。

Section IV Practical Writing: Letter of Thanks

人们在交往中常需要相互致谢，如收到别人赠送的礼物、得到别人的帮助、受到别人的慰问，都应该表示感谢。感谢信是人们常用的一种感谢方式。

感谢信的写作主要分以下三个部分：首先开头要明确地对对方提供的帮助或赠送的礼品表示谢意。主体部分则需列举对方提供的帮助，说明该帮助所起的作用，或表达对所受礼品的喜爱以及以后如何使用及收藏等。结尾部分需再次表达诚挚的谢意并问候对方。

Sample: Thanks for One's Hospitality

Directions:

Your delegation has just returned from a visit to a university in Great Britain. And you were warmly treated there by Professor Herthwell. Please write a letter to express your thanks to him for his hospitality and hope for further cooperation.

Sample

Dear Prof. Herthwell,

Many thanks for your kind hospitality and the honor you showed me during our delegation's recent visit to your university. It was nice of you to introduce me to so many famous professors and celebrated scholars at your university.

We had a safe and sound trip home. Now we have resumed our work. Again, I would like to express my warm thanks to you.

Meanwhile, I hope you will someday pay a short visit to our university and give us some lectures on Modern Western Economics.

Please have no hesitation in writing to me if you want me to do something for you in China.

Best wishes,

Li Dong

Useful expressions

1. Thank you very much /indeed for…

非常感谢……

2. I am obliged to you for your assistance during…

我很感谢你在……时的帮助

3. Thank you very much for the gift you sent me. It is one of the most wonderful gifts I got on my birthday.

非常感谢你寄给我的礼物。那是我生日那天收到最美妙的礼物之一。

4. Thanks to your effort, we had our most successful…

感谢你的努力，我们有我们最成功的……

5. Please accept my sincere thanks for your help, which I will never forget.

请接受我由衷的感谢，你对我的帮助我将永远铭记。

Practice

假设你是交换生 Tracy，刚刚结束在中国的学习，已经返回英国，请你根据以下内容用英语写一封感谢信给你的同学李华，感谢他这一学期对你的帮助及带来的美好回忆：

1. 怀念与同学们相处的快乐时光；

2. 感谢他对你汉语学习的帮助；

3. 回忆在北京游览名胜古迹的经历，感叹中华文明；

4. 表达下次还要来中国的愿望。

Practice

Dear Li Hua,

Section V Grammar: Verb（动词）

动词，就是表示动作和状态的词。根据其在句中的功能，动词可分为四类，分别是：实义动词、系动词、助动词、情态动词。

一、实义动词

实义动词又叫行为动词，分成及物动词和不及物动词。

1. 及物动词

及物动词是必须带宾语的动词，可分为如下两类。

（1）及物动词＋宾语

例：I love my home. 我爱我家。

例：He bought an English dictionary. 他买了一本英语词典。

（2）及物动词＋间接宾语＋直接宾语

例：She taught us maths. 她教我们数学。

例：My mother gave me a new pen. 母亲给了我一支新钢笔。

常用的能接双宾语的及物动词有：

give, teach, buy, lend, find, hand, leave, sell, show, read, pay, make, offer, build, pass, bring, cook 等。

2. 不及物动词

不及物动词不需要跟宾语，本身意义完整。

例：She came last week. 她上周来的。

例：It is raining hard. 正下着大雨。

例：Class began at half past seven. 7点半开始上课。

例：What happened yesterday? 昨天发生了什么事？

同一动词有时可用作及物动词，有时可用作不及物动词。

例：She can dance and sing. 她能唱歌又能跳舞。（不及物动词）

例：She can sing many English songs. 她能唱好多首英文歌曲。（及物动词）

二、系动词

系动词不能单独作谓语，后面必须跟表语构成合成式谓语。表语通常由名词、形容词，或相当于名词或形容词的词或短语等充当，说明主语是什么或怎么样。连系动词有 be, seem, look, become, get, grow, feel, appear, remain, turn。

例：The story sounds true. 这个故事听起来像是真实的。

例：Those oranges taste good. 那些橙子口感很好。

三、助动词

协助主要动词构成谓语动词词组的词叫助动词。助动词自身没有词义，不可单独使用，只能在实义动词和系动词前构成谓语的时态、语态以及否定式和疑问式。它没有对应的汉译。

例：He doesn't like English. 他不喜欢英语。（doesn't 是助动词，无词义；like 是主要动词，有词义）

四、情态动词

情态动词本身有一定的词义，表示说话人对有关行为或事物的态度和看法，认为其可能、应该或必要等，不能单独作谓语，情态动词后面加动词原形。情态动词无人称和数的变化，情态动词后面跟的动词需用原形，否定式构成是在情态动词后面加"not"。常用的情态动词有以下一些。

can（could）（能，会），例：I can swim. 我会游泳。

may（might）（可以），例：You may go now. 你现在可以走了。

must（必须），例：You must do your homework. 你必须写作业。

need（需要），例：He mecd finish that work today. 你需要今天做完这项工作。

五、动词时态

	一般时态	进行时态	完成时态	完成进行时态
现在	do/does	am/is/are doing	have/has done	have/has been doing
过去	did	was/were doing	had done	had been doing
将来	shall/will do （be going to do）	shall/will be doing	shall/will have done	shall/will have been doing
过去将来	should/would do	should/would be doing	should/would have done	should/would have been doing

六、被动语态

英语动词的语态有两种：主动语态和被动语态。主动语态表示主语是动作的执行者，被动语态表示主语是动作的承受者，在被动语态的句子中，动作的执行者一般由介词 by 引导的短语来表示。

例：We often help them. 我们常帮助他们。（主动）

例：They are often helped by us. 他们常被我们帮助。（被动）

（1）被动语态各时态的形式是由 be 动词的各时态的形式加及物动词的过去分词构成。

（2）被动语态八种时态的用法：被动语态常用的八种时态的基本用法和主动语态各时态的基本用法相同，只是句中的主语不是动作的执行者，而是动作的承受者。具体如下。

①一般现在时：谓语构成为 is/am/are done（动词的过去分词）。

例：Now English is taught in all middle schools in our country.

②一般过去时：谓语构成为 was/were done。

例：The Great Hall of the People was built in 1959.

③一般将来时：谓语构成为 will/shall be done。

例：When will the work be finished?

④过去将来时：谓语构成为 would/should be done。

例：He told us that the work would be finished the next day.

⑤现在进行时：谓语构成为 is/am/are being done。

例：Your tractor is being repaired now.

⑥过去进行时：谓语构成为 was/were being done。

例：The child was being examined by the doctor when they came in.

⑦现在完成时：谓语构成为 have/has been done。

例：The work hasn't been finished yet.

⑧过去完成时：had been done。

例：The new plan had been carried out before the second experiment began.

（3）在下列情况下，一般使用被动语态：

①当不知道动作执行者是谁或没有必要提到动作执行者时。

例：Paper was first made in China.

②当强调或突出动作承受者的作用时。

例：The new machine was invented by a 20-year-old young worker.

Exercise 1: Verb（动词）

一、单项选择

1. _____ he _____ a good rest? No, he didn't.

   A. Was, had   B. Did, had   C. Did, have   D. Do, had

2. When _____ Jim _____ the office this morning?

   A. did, get to   B. did, got to   C. did, get   D. did, got

3. _____ you _____ at seven o'clock yesterday?

   A. Do, get up   B. Did, got up   C. Do, got up   D. Did, get up

4. My father _____ a teacher. He _____ his students very much.

   A. is, like   B. is, likes   C. are, likes   D. are, like

5. His face _____ pale（苍白）when he heard the bad news.

   A. is   B. got   C. turned   D. was

6. The little girl _____ ill today.

   A. are   B. is   C. be   D. am

7. Her voice _____ like my sister's.

   A. sound   B. sounds   C. look   D. looks

8. The doctor's smile made me _____ better.

   A. felt   B. to feel   C. feeling   D. feel

9. If water _____ heated, it will be _____ into vapour.

   A. was, got   B. is, get   C. is, turned   D. was, turned

10. Lucy looks _____.

    A. happily   B. to be happy   C. happy   D. that she is happy

11. You _____ to the meeting tomorrow if you have something important to do.

    A. needn't to come   B. don't need coming

    C. don't need come   D. needn't come

12. — _____ I help you with this dress, madam?

    — Yes, I would like to try it on.

    A. May   B. Should   C. Will   D. Must

13. The only thing that really matters to the students is how soon they _____ return to their school.

A. ought to   B. must   C. have to   D. can

14. What they _____ get seems better than what they have.

A. can't   B. could   C. can   D. couldn't

15. You _____ say "thank you" when others help you.

A. should   B. must   C. needn't   D. have to

16. It's about eight o'clock. Jim _____ be here at any moment.

A. can   B. need   C. must   D. should

17. Everyone is here. _____ we start the meeting?

A. Should   B. Must   C. Can   D. Shall

18. Tom _____ the work yesterday, but he didn't.

A. should have finished   B. need have finished

C. finished   D. must have finished

19. It's known to all that you _____ lead a horse to the water but you _____ not make it drink.

A. may; can   B. will; can   C. may; dare   D. dare; can

20. You _____ come with me if you don't want to.

A. needn't   B. can't   C. mustn't   D. haven't

二、填空题

1. What time _____ your mother _____ (go) to work every day?

2. My sister _____ (enjoy) _____ (drink) coffee.

3. Health is important. You _____ (should/must) exercise more.

4. Can I _____ (park) my car here?

5. She can _____ (dance) very _____ (good).

6. The trees need _____ (water).

7. I will make all the arrangements. You _____ (need to) worry about them.

8. The story _____ (sound) terrible.

9. You are badly ill. You _____ (must/can) see a doctor.

10. I will _____ (be) back next month.

三、翻译

1. 这些玫瑰花闻起来很香。

2. 冬天来了，天气变得越来越冷了。

3. 这件连衣裙看上去很漂亮。

4. 你早餐喝牛奶么？

5. 如果你们有任何问题，请举手。

6. 我们都在等你。

7. 你必须在晚上10点前回家。

8. 明天我可以借你的相机么？

9. 我们错过了末班车，所以不得不走路回家。

10. 她一句话也没说，肯定是生气了。

Exercise 2：Tense（时态）

一、单项选择

1. Could you tell me how long have you _____ here?

   A. been   B. got   C. arrived   D. come

2. Jim has _____ to Nanjing. He will come back tomorrow.

   A. been   B. gone   C. went   D. never been

3. Lydia _____ her bag at home.

   A. leave   B. leaves   C. leaved   D. left

4. What book _____ you _____ when I _____ you at nine last night?

   A. did, read, was seeing   B. did, read, saw

   C. were, reading, saw   D. were, reading, was seeing

5. She _____ to play _____ before she was 10 years old.

   A had learned, piano   B. had learned, the piano

   C. has learned, the piano   D. learns, piano.

6. I have been studying here for three years, by next summer I _____

   A shall graduate   B graduate

   C shall be graduating   D shall be graduated

7. — _____ you ever _____ to the US?

   —Yes, twice.

   A. Have, gone   B. Have, been   C. Do, go   D. were, going

8. Mr. White was late because he _____ his way.

   A. lost   B. lose   C. loses   D. losted

9. He _____ some cooking at that time, so he _____ me.

A. did, heard
B. did, didn't hear
C. was doing, heard
D. was doing, didn't hear

10. As soon as she _____, she _____ to her roommates.

A. arrived, writes   B. arrived, written   C. arrived, wrote   D. arrived, write

11. I _____ 1000 English words by the time I was nine.

A. learnt   B. was learning   C. had learned   D. learned

12. _____ your sister _____ a book from the library?

A. Are; going to borrow
B. Is; going to borrow
C. Will; borrows
D. Are; going to borrows

13. Do you know Kate very well?

— Yes, She and I _____ friends since we were very young.

A. have made   B. have become   C. have been   D. have

14. What did you do _____?

A. just now   B. every day   C. these days   D. now

15. Could you please say it again? I _____ quite _____ you.

A. didn't, hear   B. don't, hear   C. didn't, heard   D. don't, heard

16. The angry boy went into the room and _____ the door.

A. locks   B. locking   C. lock   D. locked

17. We _____ there at nine tomorrow morning.

A. will   B. is   C. will be   D. be

18. — Let's go out to play basketball, shall we?

— OK. I _____.

A. will coming
B. be going to come
C. come
D. am coming

19. We shall go to Shanghai on business before you _____ back next month.

A. will come   B. came   C. would come   D. come

20. Look! The monkey _____ banana.

A. is eating   B. have   C. eat   D. ate

二、填空题

1. I _____ already _____ (see) the film. I _____ (see) it last Tuesday.

2. _____ you _____ (find) your English book yet?

3. His aunt has lived in China _____ (for/since) 20 days.

4. Thank you for your invitation. We _____ (enjoy) ourselves at the party last night.

5. The old lady _____ (be) ill and went to see a doctor.

6. They _____ (have) a party last night.

7. He often _____ (have) lunch at home. Today he _____ (have) lunch at school.

8. We _____ (learn) about 5000 German words by the end of last term.

9. When the president _____ (finish) speaking, he _____ (leave) the hall.

10. We _____ (leave) in a minute. We _____ (finish) all the work before we _____ (leave).

11. _____ she _____ (finish) her work today? Not yet.

12. He _____ (catch) a cold last night.

13. We _____ (visit) the museum and went home.

14. When we _____ (arrive) at the airport, he _____ (leave).

15. Lydia _____ (say) she _____ (read) the book twice.

三、翻译

1. 这些日子我们没有收到父亲的信。

2. 我们离开上海已经两年了。

3. 他去年买了一台相机。

4. 他们到英国去了。

5. 上个月我去西安旅游了。

6. 我们从未去过海南。

7. 他们到过英国。

8. 我还没读过这本书。

9. 妈妈每天都会给我买一块蛋糕。

10. 看！孩子们在操场上开心地玩耍呢。

11. 明天，我将和我的同桌去图书馆借书。

12. 火车将在两小时后到站。

13. 我把手机落在家里了。

14. 北京是中国的首都。

15. 她每天工作8个小时。

扫一扫查看
练习参考答案

扫一扫查看
本章拓展资料

Unit 4

Business Negotiation

扫一扫查看
本章教学PPT

Learning Objectives

【About Knowledge】

1. To negotiate with customers.

2. To master useful words and expressions.

3. To comprehend successful negotiation skills.

4. To know more about the Preposition.

【About Skills】

To know more about writing the letter of application.

Section 1 Dialogues

Dialogue 1

Establishing Business Relations

Ms. Zhao, the sales manager of China Arts and Crafts Trade Corporation, meets import manager Ryan from the Lenox Import Corporation of America to discuss the related issues of Chinese porcelain trade.

Ms. Zhao: Good afternoon. I'm Zhao Hui, the manager of the sales **department**.

Mr. Ryan: Good afternoon, Ms. Zhao. I'm Ryan Smith, the import manager of Lenox Import Corporation of America.

Better an open enemy than a false friend. 明枪易躲，暗箭难防。

Ms. Zhao: It's a great pleasure to meet you and we are pleased to start business with you. Have you seen our exhibits in the show room? And what **in particular you're interested in**?

Mr. Ryan: Oh, yes, we took a round yesterday and found the exhibits so **attractive**. We are especially interested in your blue and white **porcelains**.

Ms. Zhao: Great, as you know, Chinese porcelain is well known in the world and we are one of the largest porcelain exporters in China. We **used to do** business with a lot of big corporations, and I sincerely hope we can have friendly **cooperation**.

Mr. Ryan: We are one of the **leading** importers and wholesalers of Chinese porcelain. We feel confident that we can push the sale of your products in our market **as long as** you would cooperate with us on **delivery**, price, and quality.

Mr. Ryan: We shall be pleased to enter into direct business relations with you!

Vocabulary and notes

1. department: n. a division of a large organization such as a university or store that has its own function；部门，系

2. in particular: adv. specifically or especially；尤其

3. be interested in: v. show interest in something；对……感兴趣

4. attractive: adj. worth having, considering, or doing；引起兴趣的，吸引人的

5. porcelain: n. objects made of porcelain, e.g. expensive crockery or decorative figurines；瓷器

6. used to do: v. do something frequently in the past；过去常常做某事

7. cooperation: n. a situation in which people or organizations work together to achieve a result that will benefit all of them；合作

8. leading: adj. main, most important, or most successful；主要的；领导的

9. as long as: conj. used before saying the conditions that will make something else happen or be true；只要

10. delivery: n. the carrying of something such as mail, goods that have been bought, or a message to a person or address；交货

Dialogue 2

Counter offer

Mr. David, an American from a foreign trade company, is negotiating with Mr. Chou, a sales representative from Shenzhen Sunshine Import and Export Co., Ltd.

Mr. Chou: How are you this afternoon?

Mr. David: Just fine. I looked over the **catalog** you gave me this morning, and I'd like to **discuss** prices on your computer speakers.

Mr. Chou: Very good. Here is our price **list**.

Mr. David: Let me see. I see that your listed price for the K-2-1 model is ten US dollars. Do you **offer** quantity discounts?

Mr. Chou: We sure do. We give a five percent discount for orders of a hundred or more.

Mr. David: What kind of **discount** could you give me if I were to **place an order** for six hundred units?

Mr. Chou: On an order of six hundred, we can give you a discount of ten percent.

Mr. David: What about the **lead time**?

Mr. Chou: We could **ship** your order within ten days when receiving your payment.

Mr. David: So, you **require** payment in advance of shipment?

Mr. Chou: Yes. You could transfer the payment into our bank account or open a letter of credit in our favor.

Mr. David: I'd like to place an order for six hundred units.

Mr. Chou: Great! I'll just fill out the **purchase** order and give you to sign it.

Vocabulary and notes

1. catalog: n. a list of priced and illustrated items for sale, presented in book form or in other formats including CD-ROM or video；目录册

2. discuss: n. to talk about a subject with others；讨论

3. list: n. a series of related words, names, numbers, or other items that are arranged in order, one after the other；清单

4. offer: v. to provide something, or make something available for those who want it；提供

5. discount: n. a reduction in the usual price of something；折扣

6. place an order: v. request a company to supply goods；下订单；订购

7. lead time: the time needed to do something measured from start to finish; e.g. from design to production or from placing an order to delivery of the goods；订货交付时间

8. ship: v. to transport something by ship；运输；装船

9. require: v. order; demand；要求

10. purchase: n. to buy something using money or its equivalent；采购；购买

Dialogue 3

Negotiating the prices

Dan Smith, from a foreign trade company, is negotiating with Ms. Li about the prices.

Mr. Dan: I'd like to get the ball rolling by talking about prices.

Ms. Li: I'd be happy to answer any questions you may have.

Mr. Dan: Your products are very good. But I'm a little worried about the prices you're asking.

Ms. Li: You think our offer is too high?

Mr. Dan: That's not **exactly** what I had in **mind**. I know your research costs are high, but what I'd like is a 25% discount.

Ms. Li: That seems to be a little high, Mr. Smith. I don't know how we can **make a profit** with those numbers.

Mr. Dan: Please, Ms. Li, call me Dan. Well, if we promise a lasting business relationship, volume sales will slash your costs for making the products, right?

Ms. Li: Yes, but it's hard to see how you can place such large orders. How could you turn over so many? We'd need a **guarantee** of future business, not just a **promise**.

Mr. Dan: We said we wanted 1000 pieces over a six-month period. **What if** we place orders for twelve months, with a guarantee?

Ms. Li: If you can guarantee that on paper, I think we can discuss this further.

Vocabulary and notes

1. exactly: adv. used to emphasize that a particular quality or quantity is stated precisely；完全地

2. mind: n. the center of consciousness that generates thoughts, feelings, ideas, and perceptions, and stores knowledge and memories；心中

3. make a profit: v. gain money by selling goods or doing business；获利

4. guarantee: v. to promise something, or make something certain；保证

5. promise: v. to assure somebody that something will certainly happen or be done；允诺；承诺

6. what if: v. used to ask what you should do or what the result will be if something happens, especially something unpleasant；要是……

Dialogue 4

Signing the Contract

Mr. Carl is talking about the terms of the contract with Mr. Chou to reach the agreement.

Mr. Carl: Now that we have agreed on all the matters, let's sign the contract. Please go over it and see if everything is **in order**.

Mr. Chou: Okay. Let me read it over. Don't you think we should add a sentence here like this: if one side **fails** to **observe** the contract, the other side **is entitled to** cancel it, and the loss for this reason should be **charged** by the side **breaking the contract**.

Mr. Carl: That's OK. I think all the **terms** should meet with unanimous agreement. Do you have any comment on this **clause**?

Mr. Chou: It is acceptable, but the time of payment should be **prolonged** 2 to 3 months.

Mr. Carl: Usually we are accustomed to payment within one month, but **for the sake of** the friendship between us, we'll fix it at two months.

Mr. Chou: You are so considerate. No wonder everyone **speaks highly of** your commercial integrity.

Mr. Carl: Thank you for your **compliment**. You know, it is our permanent principle that contracts are honored and commercial **integrity** is maintained. Anything else you want to bring up for discussion ?

Mr. Chou: Yes, one more thing I would like to point out, that is timely delivery. You know our customers are in urgent need of the goods. If you fail to deliver the goods at the time stipulated in the contract, they may turn elsewhere for substitution. By the way, we just can't **stand the loss**.

Mr. Carl: Well, we can assure you that the shipment will be duly delivered.

Mr. Chou: I think we have no questions about the terms. We can sign the contract now. I'm glad our negotiation has come to a successful conclusion. I hope this will **lead to** further business between us.

Vocabulary and notes

1. in order: adj. in a correct sequence or arrangement；秩序井然

2. fail: v. to be unsuccessful in trying to do something；失败

3. observe: v. to carry out or comply with something such as a law or custom；遵守

4. be entitled to: v. have the right to do something；有权做……

5. charge: v. to ask somebody for an amount of money as a price or fee；要价；收费

6. break the contract: v. fail to observe the contract；违约

7. terms: n. the requirements laid down formally in an agreement or contract, or proposed by one side when negotiating an agreement；条款

8. clause: n. a part of a legal document or law that officially states that something must be done；条款

9. prolong: v. to make something go on longer；延长

10. for the sake of: adv. for the benefit or good of someone or something；为了……起见

11. speak highly of: v. praise；赞扬

12. compliment: n. something said to express praise or approval；赞美

13. integrity: n. the quality of always behaving according to the moral principles that you believe in, so that people respect and trust you；诚实正直

14. stand the loss: v. sustain loss；承受损失

15. lead to: v. cause；导致

Activity

Make up a dialogue based on the following situation.

Suppose you are a salesman from Beijing Sunrise Foreign Trade Company, you're going to negotiate with Mr. Ryan, a sales manager from a foreign trade company, about the price of the products, the package and shipment to reach an agreement.

Section II *Extensive Reading*

Passage 1

On Business Negotiation Etiquette and Skills

With the development（发展）of economy, international communication is becoming more and more frequent in China and **etiquette** also becomes an essential part of our social life. Business negotiation is business communication events among enterprises and the quality of negotiators will directly **affect** the success or failure of the negotiation. This essay **focuses on** the etiquette（礼仪）in business negotiation.

Negotiation etiquette can be divided into language etiquette and non-verbal etiquette. Language is the **exchange** of information of human symbolic systems. Negotiating language should be both **appropriate** and **courteous**. In addition, non-verbal communication is not to convey meaning through the oral language, but from **body language**. Non-verbal rituals, including ritual gaze, facial expression etiquette, gesture rituals and silent etiquette. Non-verbal etiquette is a real art, because different countries have different cultures. For instance, in China, US and Canada, nodding means "agree", however, in Bulgaria and Nepal, it means "do not agree" and in Japan, it just means "understanding" but not "consent".

Let us look at an example of British businessman in Iran: In this month, everything is successful and he **gets along well with** colleagues（同事）in Iran and respects the traditions of Islam to avoid any explosive political words. After he signed the contact, he gave his colleague of Persia the thumbs up. Almost immediately, an official of Iran left the room. The British businessman couldn't understand what happened and his Iranian masters also felt embarrassed and didn't know how to explain it. The fact is that in England, a thumbs-up is the symbol of agreement and means "excellent". However, in Iran, it means negation and dissatisfaction and it's a rude action.

With the rapid development of our society, more and more **competitions** arise in business. People usually increase business negotiation to get **opportunities** and cooperation. Business negotiation is a challenging communication activity, which requires the parties to recognize the truth, identify the purpose, and master the negotiating essentials. Business negotiation can deepen the ability of understanding to make better communication（交流）and cooperation. Negotiation etiquette is an **indispensable** part during the business negotiation. But due to the cultural differences, the negotiation etiquette is different. As a successful negotiator, no matter what kind of culture we face, an appropriate etiquette is significant and meaningful. In a word, we should be familiar with different cultures and customs of all countries and make full preparation before the negotiation to avoid embarrassment and misunderstanding.

Vocabulary and notes

1. etiquette: n. a set of rules for behaving correctly in social situations；礼仪

2. affect: v. to act upon or have an effect on somebody or something；影响

3. focus on: v. come together at a focus；聚焦于；集中于

4. exchange: n. to give something and receive something different in return；交换

5. appropriate: adj. suitable or right for a particular situation or purpose；合适的

6. courteous: adj. polite in a way that shows consideration of others or good manners；有礼貌的

7. body language: n. the movements or positions of your body that show other people what you are thinking or feeling；肢体语言

8. get along well with: v. to be in harmony with others 与……相处融洽

9. competition: n. the process of trying to win or do better than others；竞争

10. opportunity: n. a chance, especially one that offers some kind of advantage；机会；机遇

11. indispensable: adj. difficult or impossible to exist without or to do sth. 必不可少的

12. Business negotiation is business communication events among enterprises and the quality of negotiators will directly affect the success or failure of the negotiation. This essay focuses on the etiquette in business negotiation. 商务谈判是企业间的商务交流活动，谈判人员的素

质将直接影响谈判的成败。本文主要探讨商务谈判中的礼仪问题。

13. For instance, in China, US and Canada, nodding means "agree", however, in Bulgaria and Nepal, it means "do not agree" and in Japan, it just means "understanding" but not "consent". 例如，在中国、美国和加拿大，点头的意思是"同意"，而在保加利亚和尼泊尔，点头的意思是"不同意"；在日本，点头的意思是"理解"，而不是"同意"。

14. Business negotiation is a challenging communication activity, which requires the parties to recognize the truth, identify the purpose, and master the negotiating essentials. 商务谈判是一项富有挑战性的交际活动，它要求双方认清事实，明确目的，掌握谈判要领。

 译文

论商务谈判礼仪与技巧

随着经济的发展，国际交流在中国越来越频繁，礼仪也成为我们社会生活中不可或缺的一部分。商务谈判是企业间的商务交流活动，谈判人员的素质将直接影响谈判的成败。本文主要探讨商务谈判中的礼仪问题。

谈判礼仪可分为语言礼仪和非言语礼仪。语言是人类符号系统的信息交换。谈判语言应该既恰当又礼貌。非言语交际通过肢体语言而非通过口头语言来传达意思。非言语仪式，包括仪式凝视、面部表情礼仪、手势仪式和沉默礼仪。非言语礼仪是一门真正的艺术，因为不同的国家有不同的文化。例如，在中国、美国和加拿大，点头的意思是"同意"，而在保加利亚和尼泊尔，点的意思是"不同意"；在日本，点头的意思是"理解"，而不是"同意"。

让我们看一个英国商人在伊朗的例子：在这个月里，一切都很成功，他与伊朗的同事相处融洽，尊重伊斯兰教的传统，以避免任何具有爆炸性的政治言论。在合同上签字后，他对着他的波斯同事竖起了大拇指。一名伊朗官员立马离开了房间。这位英国商人不明白发生了什么，他的伊朗主人也感到很尴尬，不知道如何解释。事实上，在英国，竖起大拇指表示同意，意思是"优秀"。然而，在伊朗，这意味着否定和不满，这是一种粗鲁的行为。

随着社会的快速发展，商业竞争越来越激烈。人们通常通过增加商务谈判来获得机会和合作。商务谈判是一项富有挑战性的交际活动，它要求双方认清事实，明确目的，掌握谈判要领。商务谈判可以加深理解能力，更好地进行沟通与合作。谈判礼仪是商务谈判中不可缺少的一部分。但由于文化差异，谈判礼仪也有所不同。作为一个成功的谈判者，无论我们面对什么样的文化，适当的礼仪是有意义的。总之，我们应该熟悉各国不同的文化和风俗习惯，在谈判前做好充分准备，避免尴尬和误解。

📖 Passage 2

TIMBER SALE CONTRACT—— SAMPLE

The following document（文件）offers excellent guidelines when preparing a timber sale contract. Separate **articles** may be added to suit **specific** circumstances. It is advised that the Seller and Purchaser employ legal counsel to review the contract prior to its **endorsement**.

Contract entered into this _____ day of _____, 20___, by and between _____ of _____ Illinois, hereinafter（以下）called the Seller, and _____, of _____ (city), _____ (state), Illinois Timber Buyer License Number _____, hereinafter called the Purchaser.

1. The Seller agrees to sell and the Purchaser agrees to buy for the total sum of _____ dollars ($_____) under the conditions set forth in this contract all of the live standing timber marked or designated for cutting and all of the dead or down timber marked or designated upon an area of approximately _____ acres, situated in the _____ of Section _____, _____ County, Illinois, on land owned and recorded in the name of _____.

The Purchaser further agrees to pay to the Seller as an **initial payment** under this contract the sum of _____ dollars ($_____), receipt of which is hereby acknowledged, and a final payment in the sum of _____ dollars（$_____), prior to any cutting or removal of timber under this contract.

2. The Seller further agrees to mark and dispose of the timber conveyed in this contract in strict accordance with the following conditions（条件）：

（a）All trees to be included in this sale will be marked with a **distinctive** mark on the bole and stump of each tree.

（b）No trees under _____ inches in diameter at a point 4½ feet from the ground will be marked for cutting.

(c) No concurrent contract involving (包含) the area or period **covered** in this contract has been or will be entered into by the Seller without the **written consent** of the Purchaser.

(d) The Purchaser and his employees shall have access to the area at all reasonable times and seasons for the purpose of **carrying out** the terms of this contract.

(e) Unless otherwise specified, all material contained in the marked or designated trees is included in this sale.

3. The Purchaser (买家) further agrees to cut and remove all of the timber conveyed in this contract in strict accordance with the following conditions:

(a) Unless an extension of time is agreed upon in writing between the Seller and Purchaser, all timber shall be paid for, cut, and removed on or before and none after the _____ day of _____, 20___, and any material not so removed shall **revert** to the Seller.

(b) Unmarked trees and young timber shall be protected against unnecessary injury from felling and logging operations. If, however, unmarked trees are cut, damages shall be paid the Seller at the rate of $1 per square fort per tree. for all other species, and in the event that any such trees are cut, said trees shall remain upon the premises and shall be the property of the Seller.

(c) Necessary logging roads shall be cleared by the Purchaser only after their locations have been definitely agreed upon with the Seller or his representative, and any trees to be removed in the clearing operations shall first be marked by the Seller.

(d) During the life of this contract and on the area covered, care shall be exercised by the Purchaser and his employees against the starting and spread of fire, and they shall do all in their power to prevent and control fires.

(e) Any liability (责任) for damage, destruction, or restoration of private or public improvements or personal damages occasioned by or in the exercise of this contract shall be the sole responsibility of the Purchaser, and the Purchaser shall save harmless the Seller **on account of** such damages.

(f) The risk if loss or damage to the trees herein purchased, from any and all causes whatever, shall be borne by purchasers from the date hereof.

(g) The Purchaser will not assign this agreement without the written consent of the Seller.

4. The Seller and Purchaser mutually agree as follows:

(a) All modifications of the contract will be reduced to writing, dated, signed, and witnessed and attached to this contract.

（b）Any need for reassignment of interest of either party may be changed within 10 days following written consent by both parties. All terms of this contract legally bind the named representatives to excuse this document as written.

（c）The total number of trees conveyed is _____ (having a volume of approximately _____ bd. ft.) composed as follows:

_____ white oak, _____ red and black oak, _____, _____, _____, _____.

（d）In case of **dispute** over the terms of this contract, final decision shall rest with a reputable person to be mutually agreed upon the by parties to this contract. If the parties hereto do not **agree upon** a third party within 10 days following the initiation of the dispute, or **in case of** further disagreement, then within 15 days from the initiation of the dispute, it shall be submitted to a Board of Arbitration of three persons, one to be selected by each party to this contract and the third to be selected by the other two. The Board shall decide the dispute within 5 days after the matter is referred to it.

In the event that damages（损害）are **awarded** to the Seller by the Board of Arbitration and are not paid on the date that the award is made, then all operations of the Purchaser shall immediately cease, and if the award is not paid or satisfied within 30 days after the date of award, the Seller may take immediate possession of the premises upon which the timber is located, shall retain as liquidated damages all money paid by the Purchaser, and the title to all timber shall revert to and become the property of the seller.

In witness whereof, the parties hereto have set their hands and seals this _____ day of _____, 20____.

WITNESSES:

_____

for the Purchaser

_____

for the Seller

_____

Vocabulary and notes

1. articles: n. a section of a legal document that deals with a specific point；条款

2. specific: adj. precise and detailed, avoiding vagueness；明确的；具体的

3. endorsement: n. an act or instance of endorsing a check or other financial document；签署

4. initial payment: n. 初付费

5. distinctive: adj. uniquely characteristic of a person, group, or thing；独特的

6. cover: n. to lie across or in a layer over the whole of or the upper surface of something；包括；覆盖

7. written consent: n. 书面同意

8. carry out: v. to complete a task or activity；实施；执行

9. revert: v. to become once again the property of the former owner or his or her heirs；归属

10. on account of: n. because of；因为

11. dispute: n. a serious argument or disagreement；纠纷

12. agree upon: v. agree；赞成

13. in case of: n. 万一

14. award: v. to bestow, grant, or assign something to somebody by a judicial decision or by arbitration；裁定；判给

15. The Purchaser and his employees shall have access to the area at all reasonable times and seasons for the purpose of carrying out the terms of this contract. 为执行本合同条款，买方及其雇员可在所有合理时间和季节进入该区域。

16. Any liability for damage, destruction, or restoration of private or public improvements or personal damages occasioned by or in the exercise of this contract shall be the sole responsibility of the Purchaser, and the Purchaser shall save harmless the Seller on account of such damages. 因履行本合同或在履行本合同过程中对私人或公共设施造成的损坏、破坏或恢复或个人损害的任何责任应由买方全权负责，买方应保护卖方免受此类损害。

译文

木材销售合同——样本

以下文本为准备木材销售合同提供了很好的指导。可根据具体情况另行增加条款。建议卖方和买方在签署合同前聘请法律顾问对合同进行审查。

伊利诺伊州 _____（城市），（以下简称为"卖方"）与 _____（州）_____（市）。（县），伊利诺伊州木材购买者许可证编号 _____（以下简称"买方"）签订合同，合同签订日期为 20 ___，_____。

1. 本合同规定条件下，卖方同意出售，买方同意购买的总金额为 _____ 美元（$ _____），交易物品为标记或指定用于切割的所有活立木以及标记或指定的所有废旧或砍伐木材，这些木材所在区域将近 _____ 英亩，位于 _____ 地区，伊利诺伊州 _____ 县，以 _____ 的名义拥有并记录在案。

买方同意在此之前向卖方支付 _____ 美元（$ _____）的金额作为本合同的初始付款，并在此确认收据，按本合同规定进行砍伐木材前将会支付 _____ 美元（$ _____）的余款。

2. 卖方同意严格按照以下条件对本合同中转让的木材进行标记和处理：

（a）本次销售中的所有树木的树干和树桩上将做一个独特的标记。

（b）距离地面 4½ 英尺处，直径在 _____ 英寸以下的树木不会被标记为砍伐。

（c）未经买方书面同意，卖方已经或将要订立涉及本合同涵盖区域或期限的并行合同无效。

（d）为执行本合同条款，买方及其雇员可在所有合理时间和季节进入该区域。

（e）除非另有规定，标记或指定树木中包含的所有材料均包含在本次销售中。

3. 买方还同意严格按照以下条件切割和移除本合同中转让的所有木材：

（a）除非买卖双方以书面形式约定延长时间，否则所有木材均应在 _____ 日，20 ___，_____ 日或之前付款，砍伐和移走，尚未清除的所有木材应归还卖方。

（b）未经标记的树木和幼龄木材应受到保护，以免因采伐和伐木作业而受到不必要的伤害。但是，如果未标记的树木被砍伐，买方应按照每棵树每平方英尺 1 美元的价格为所有其他物种向卖方支付损害赔偿金，如果任何此类树木被砍伐，则上述树木应保留在该区域内，并应归属为卖方的财产。

（c）买方应在与卖方或其代表明确商定必要的伐木道路的位置后进行清理，清理作业中需要移除的任何树木应首先由卖方标记。

（d）在本合同有效期内和所覆盖区域内，买方及其员工应注意防止火灾的发生和蔓延，并应尽其所能预防和控制火灾。

（e）因履行本合同或在履行本合同过程中对私人或公共设施造成的损坏、破坏或恢复或个人损害的任何责任应由买方全权负责，买方应保护卖方免受此类损害。

（f）从本合同签订之日起，因任何原因造成的树木损失或损坏的风险应由买方承担。

（g）未经卖方书面同意，买方不得转让本协议。

4. 买卖双方相互同意如下：

（a）对合同的所有修改将简化为书面形式，注明日期，签署，见证并附加在本合同上。

（b）在双方书面同意后的10天内，任一方可以根据需要更改利益赋值。本合同的所有条款均具有法律约束力，指定的代表应按所列条款解释本文件。

（c）转让的树木总数为_____（体积约为　　　　板英尺），组成如下：

_____ 白色橡木，_____ 红色和黑色橡木，_____，_____，_____，_____。

（d）如果对本合同条款有争议，最终决定权在本合同双方共同商定的信誉良好的人员。如果本合同双方在争议开始后10天内未能就第三方达成一致意见，或在进一步分歧的情况下，应在争议开始后15天内，将争议提交由三人组成的仲裁委员会，其中两人由本合同各方选定，第三人由另外两人选定。委员会应在该事项提交委员会后5天内对争议做出裁决。

如果仲裁委员会裁决卖方损害赔偿金，但在裁决做出之日仍未支付，则买方的所有经营活动应立即停止，如果在裁决后30天内未支付或未履行裁决，卖方可立即占有木材所在地，应保留买方支付的所有款项作为违约赔偿金，所有木材的所有权应归卖方所有。

双方已于20____年____月____日盖章，以资证明。

证人：

_____

买方：

_____

卖方：

_____

Section III Case Analysis in Intercultural Communication

Equality or Hospitality for Table Manners

Lin Hua has accompanied an American delegation to visit China. They have experienced the hospitality of the Chinese people. After returning to America, Lin Hua once visited them. They were so glad to meet again. Lin Hua offered to host the meal, but they refused. They ordered their own dish, and Lin Hua ordered her own. When footing the bill, they only paid their part, and no one wanted to pay for Lin Hua. Lin Hua found them so inhospitable, though she knew the Americans would usually pay for their own food.

Question for discussion

Why did Lin Hua find them inhospitable?

分析：

（1）在中国，为了表示好客，人们倾向于招待客人。如果他们做不到这一点，他们至少会努力为客人买单。

（2）在美国，人们倾向于为自己买单，以显示平等和独立。

（3）林华知道这个习俗，但从中国人的角度来看，她还是觉得很难接受，觉得有点冷漠。因此，需了解不同文化之间的差异，培养对文化差异的敏感性，学会与来自不同文化背景的人进行交流，发展跨文化意识，已成为新时代的迫切需求。

Section IV Practical Writing: Letter of Application

申请信有很多种，比如求职申请、加入某组织或活动的申请、报考申请、留学申请等。由于此类题目常有较多的文字提示，写作时除应注意格式上的要求外，也应注意审题全面，不能遗漏要点。具体写作结构为：

申请信
- 点明写信目的，自我介绍，点出信息来源
- 详述个人优势，简述个人要求
- 表达感谢，简述获准后的打算，期盼批准

Sample

Dear sir,

    Please consider me as an applicant for the position of accountant which you recently advertised in China Daily. I am twenty-four years old and I will graduate from the university this July.

    I am majoring in accounting. during the four years study, I've got a very good academic score. And also when I was a junior, I once had a part time job in the local accounting firm because I felt that an academic education in a field such as accounting can be enhanced tremendously by contact with professionals in the field. I did my work well.

    I would be grateful for the opportunity to put what I've learned in the college into real use and discuss my accounting experience and any other aspects of my background that the enclosed resume does not cover. Could we meet at your convenience? I would greatly appreciate a personal interview. Please call me any day from 8:00-22:00 at the number 62778888 or write to me to the address on the envelop.

Yours truly,
Wang Ning

Useful expressions

（一）开头常用语

1. I learned on your website that…

我从你们的网站上得知……

2. I'm writing to apply for the job/post/position as…

我写信申请……的工作缺位。

3. I am writing this letter to recommend myself as qualified candidate for…

我写信推荐自己为……的合格人选。

（二）主体部分常用语

1. As an outgoing…get along well with my classmates.

作为一名外向的……我和同学们相处得很好。

2. For one thing, I can help…For another, I can improve my English, make more friends,

and enrich my life.

一方面，我能帮助……另一方面，我能提高我的英语水平，结交更多的朋友，丰富我的生活。

3. I am confident that I'm suitable for/qualified to do/equal to (doing) something.

我确信，我适合……/ 我有做……的资格 / 我能胜任（做）某事。

（三）结尾常用语

1. I would greatly appreciate it if you could take my application into consideration.

如果您能考虑我的申请，我将不胜感激。

2. If you offer me an interview opportunity, I would be most grateful. Look forward to your reply soon.

如果您能给我提供面试机会，我将非常感激。期待您的早日答复。

Practice

假定你是李华，将于今年七月从新星外语学校毕业，你从报纸上得知 B&B 公司要招聘一名英文秘书，你很感兴趣，请给该公司写一封求职信，包括下列要求：年龄；学习情况及英语水平；兴趣和特长；性格特点。

注意：1. 词数 100 词左右；

2. 可以适当增加细节，使行文连贯；

3. 开头语和结束语已为你写好。

Practice

Dear Sirs,

I'm looking forward to your reply.

Sincerely Yours,

Li Hua

Section V Grammar: Preposition（介词）

介词是用来表明名词、代词等与句中其他词的关系的。介词是虚词，不能重读，不能单独作句子成分，需要和它后面的词共同充当句子成分。介词后面的名词、代词或相当于名词的部分称为介词宾语，简称介宾。下面简单介绍简单介词和复合介词的用法。

一、介词的种类

1. 简单介词

常用的有 at, in, on, about, across, before, beside, for , to, without, to, by, with, of, over, behind, up, after, against 等。

2. 复合介词

如 onto, along with, because of, in front of, instead of 等。

3. 介词和其他词类的习惯搭配

（1）和动词的搭配，如 agree with, ask for, belong to, keep away from, care about 等。

（2）和形容词的搭配，如 afraid of, angry with, different from, good at 等。

（3）和名词的搭配，如 answer to, key to, reason for, visit to 等。

＊介词后常跟人称代词的宾格和动词的 ing 形式。

二、某些介词的意义与用法区别

1. at, on, in（表时间）

at 表示时间的一点；in 表示一个时期；on 表示特殊日子

（1）at 后常接几点几分，天明，中午，日出，日落，开始等。如：

at five o'clock（五点），at down（黎明），at daybreak（天亮），at sunrise（日出），at noon（中午），at sunset（日落），at midnight（半夜），at the beginning of the month（月初），at that time（那时），at that moment（那会儿），at this time of day（在一天的这个时候）。

（2）in 后常接年，月，日期，上午，下午，晚上，白天，季节，世纪等。如：

in 2006（2006 年），in May（5 月），2004（2004 年五月），in the morning（早晨/上午），in the afternoon（下午），in the evening（晚上），in the night（夜晚），in the daytime（白天），in the 21st century（21 世纪），in three days（weeks/month）三天（周/个月），in a week（一周），in spring（春季）。

（3）on 后跟某日，星期几，某日的朝夕，节日等，即具体某一天及其早、中、晚。如：

on Sunday（星期日），on a warm morning in April（四月的一个温暖的上午），on a December night（12月的一个夜晚），on that afternoon（那天下午），on the following night（下一个晚上），on Christmas afternoon（圣诞节下午），on October 1, 1949（1949年10月1日），on New Year's Day（春节）。

特别提示：在 last, next, this, that, some, every 等词之前一律不用介词。

2. between, among（表位置）"在……之间"

（1）between 仅用于二者之间，但说三者或三者以上中的每两个之间的相互关系时，也可用 between。

例：I'm sitting between Tom and Alice.

例：The village lies between three hills.

（2）among 用于三者或三者以上之间。

例：He is the best among the students.

3. beside, besides, except

（1）beside 意为"在……旁边"。

例：He sat beside me.

（2）besides 意为"除……之外"，包括在内。

例：What do you want besides this?

（3）except 意为"除……之外"，不包括在内。

例：They go to work in a week except Saturday.

4. in the tree, on the tree

（1）in the tree，指动物或人等外来的东西在树上。

（2）on the tree，指果实或叶子等树本身长出来的东西。

5. on the way, by the way, in this way

（1）on the way 指在路上，on one's way to…

（2）by the way 指顺便问一句。

（3）in this way 用这样的方法，in that way，in other way，in these ways。

6. by bus, on the bus

（1）by bus 是一般说法，固定搭配。

（2）on the bus 特指乘某一辆车

7. across, through, past

（1）across 从表面经过，如：road，bridge，river。

（2）through 从内部空间经过，如：city，woods，forests，window，gate。

（3）past 从旁边经过。

Exercise 1：Preposition（介词）

一、单项选择

1. This is a map _____ Russia.
A. to   B. at   C. of   D. on

2. A group _____ boys and girls are running on the track.
A. in   B. of   C. for   D. to

3. China is famous _____ the Great Wall.
A. as   B. of   C. to   D. for

4. These spoons are made _____ metal and wood.
A. of   B. from   C. by   D. in

5. My English teacher often mistakes me _____ my twin sister.
A. to   B. as   C. for   D. with

6. The English teacher is not only strict _____ his students but also strict _____ his own work.
A. with; in   B. in; in   C. in; with   D. with; with

7. We go to work _____ bike.
A. in   B. by   C. at   D. on

8. My mother will come _____ four days.
A. in   B. after   C. before   D. later

9. She went to Nanjing and returned _____ four days.
A. after   B. before   C. later   D. in

10. The boss will be back _____ four o'clock.
A. after   B. in   C. on   D. at

11. China built the Great Wall _____ the northern part _____ the country to protect avoid being attacked.

A. to; in   B. across; on   C. across; of   D. at; of

12. Michael always comes late _____ work.

A. to   B. inside   C. at   D. for

13. It's cold _____ winter in Tianjin.

A. by   B. on   C. at   D. in

14. The girl _____ a red coat is my sister.

A. in   B. at   C. of   D. on

15. Finally we agreed _____ the terms of the contract.

A. at   B. to   C. with   D. on

16. Do you often hear _____ your classmate?

A. about   B. from   C. out of   D. of

17. The doctor is busy _____ performing an operation.

A. with   B. for   C. on   D. of

18. My teacher was angry _____ me _____ my being late.

A. at; for   B. at; with   C. with; for   D. with; about

19. The trees _____ front of the house is _____ the charge of Mr. Wang.

A. in; by   B. from; in   C. in; in   D. at; in

20. I remember Lucy left _____ a very bitter cold morning of December.

A. from   B. on   C. at   D. in

二、填空题

1. I'm really sorry. I can't say it _____ English.

2. Is anyone _____ home?

3. There is a big hole _____ the wall.

4. It's 10 p.m. It's time for us to go _____ bed.

5. What's wrong _____ your face?

6. They usually have lunch _____ the middle of the day.

7. I often help my little brother _____ his math.

8. What are you talking _____?

9. I'm afraid she is _____ the office _____ the moment.

10. The girl is asking her teacher _____ the English song contest.

11. Are Michael and Lucy _____ the same group?

12. Could you pass the spoon _____ me?

13. Put the book _____ there.

14. May I borrow a notebook _____ you?

15. I have a lot _____ housework to do every Sunday.

16. She is sitting _____ front of the store.

17. Did you live _____ Nanjing in 2000?

18. I think Lily is _____ duty today.

19. Thanks _____ asking me to your birthday party.

20. My camera is different _____ yours.

三、翻译

1. 期末考试不难，不要担心。

2. 我对他的所作所为很气愤。

3. 学校离我家只有 1 公里。

4. 休息的时间到了。

5. 没有你的帮助，我不可能成功。

6. 台湾在福建省的东南方。

7. 桌上的笔是我的。

8. 河流经这座城市。

9. 我把钱放进口袋然后离开超市。

10. 春天百花齐放。

11. 我坐在教室的前半部分。

12. 我必须在下午 3 点前完成家庭作业。

13. 我们每天早上 7 点吃早餐。

14. 音乐对很多人来说很重要。

15. 感谢你邀请我参加你的婚礼。

16. 丽丽害怕独自待着。

17. 中华人民共和国成立于 1949 年。

18. 因为贫困，很多孩子辍学了。

19. 父母对我的表现非常满意。

20. 超市的后面有一棵树。

扫一扫查看
练习参考答案

扫一扫查看
本章拓展资料

Module 2
Innovation and Entrepreneurship

Unit 5

Innovation

📱 Learning Objectives

【About Knowledge】

1. To understand the meaning of innovation.

2. To master useful words and expressions.

3. To comprehend the spirits of innovation.

4. To know more about sentence composition and main sentence structures.

【About Skills】

To know more about writing the posts.

Section I *Dialogues*

📖 Dialogue 1

The Importance of Innovation

Ms. Zhao, a college teacher, is talking with her students about the topic "Do you think innovation is important to college students? How can college students foster innovation?"

Ms. Zhao: Boys and girls, do you think **innovation** is important to us college students?

Student A, B and C: Of course.

Student A: If you only do things as other people tell you, you don't **embrace** the innovation. Although your achievement is very perfect, it can't attract any company to employ you.

Ms. Zhao: Maybe it is because nowadays corporations think innovation is more important than **technical** skill. But what should we do to foster our innovation?

Student B: I think we should cultivate innovation in students **as earlier as possible**. And the more books you read, the larger your field of **vision** opens. **Accumulate** enough knowledge and you will develop innovative ability sooner.

Student A: What about you?

Student C: I think the best way to cultivate innovation is to arouse students' **curiosity**. When students are curious, they will be interested in learning and searching, just like children. Teachers shouldn't ignore or laugh at their ideas which might be silly, because you will **snuff out** their curiosity.

Student A: I agree with you. Maybe the parents should lead them to think in a different but reasonable way.

Student B: Also, I think the school should train their independent thinking ability.

Student C: In the meantime, the society should create an atmosphere in encouraging innovation.

Ms. Zhao: In a brief, for ourselves, we should keep us full of curiosity and learning new knowledge.

Vocabulary and notes

1. innovation: n. the act or process of inventing or introducing something new；创新；改革；（新事物、思想或方法的）创造；新思想

2. embrace: v. a situation in which someone completely accepts something such as a new belief, idea, or way of life；包括；欣然接受；包含

3. technical: adj. relating to or specializing in industrial techniques or subjects or applied science；技术的；技能的；工艺的；专门技术的

4. as earlier as possible: 尽早

5. vision: n. an image or series of images seen in a dream or trance, often interpreted as having religious, revelatory, or prophetic significance；视野；视力；异象；想象

6. accumulate: v. to collect or obtain a large amount of something over a period of time；积累；积聚；（数量）逐渐增加

7. curiosity: n. eagerness to know about something or to get information；好奇心；求知

欲；珍品

8. snuff: v. to extinguish a flame; e.g. that of a burning candle；掐灭

9. snuff out: 吹熄（蜡烛等）；压灭（希望等）；扫除；扑灭

📖 Dialogue 2

Innovation and Entrepreneurship Competition

Ann is discussing with her roommates about the innovation and entrepreneurship competition.

Ann: The school is going to hold the "Innovation and **Entrepreneurship** Competition". we can **sign up** for the competition together.

Betty: What is innovation and entrepreneurship competition?

Ann: This year's **competition** is based on the **theme** of "'Internet Plus' to achieve dreams, 'innovation and entrepreneurship' to open up the future", hoping to **inspire** our college students' creativity.

Lucy: What is the form of the competition?

Ann: It is to explain our innovation and entrepreneurship ideas in the form of a speech with PPT. I have an innovative idea. How about opening a travel agency?

Elaine: There are also many travel **agencies** in China. What are our innovations?

Ann: We can develop the "love tourism market". Newlyweds generally have more **discretionary** income and time than **ordinary couples**. Our love tourism can cover: a trip of the first meeting, honeymoon, a golden and silver wedding anniversary, and a romantic wedding dress tour.

Betty: We can set up a love festival to attract tourists, like the birth of Single Day of Taobao.

Lucy: At the end of the tour, we will make **the unforgettable memories** of the couples into DV or a photo album and give them to the travelers for free to win the regular customers.

Elaine: These ideas are really creative. Let's sign up for the competition.

Vocabulary and notes

1. entrepreneurship: n. the state of being an entrepreneur, or the activities associated with

being an entrepreneur；企业家精神；工商企业家

2. sign up: to agree to participate in something, or get somebody to agree to participate in something, especially by way of a signature；注册；报名；签约

3. competition: n. an activity in which people try to win something or do better than others；竞争；比赛；竞赛；对手

4. theme: n. the subject of a discourse, discussion, piece of writing, or artistic composition；主题；主旋律

5. inspire: v. to encourage somebody to greater effort, enthusiasm, or creativity；激励；鼓舞；赋予灵感；引起联想

6. agency: n. an organization, especially a company, that acts as the agent, representative, or subcontractor of a person or another company；服务机构；经销机构

7. discretionary: adj. giving somebody the freedom to make a decision according to individual circumstances；自行决定的；酌情行事的；便宜行事的

8. ordinary: adj. not remarkable or special in any way, and therefore uninteresting and unimpressive；普通的；平常的；一般的；平凡的

9. couple: n. two people who are married, are living together, or have an intimate relationship；情侣；夫妇；两人

10. the unforgettable memories: 难忘的回忆

📖 Dialogue 3

Negotiating the prices

Ann and her roommates are sharing their experience learned from the innovation and entrepreneurship competition. They are very happy with the result.

Ann: My God, we won **the first prize** of the college innovation and entrepreneurship competition. We are so happy to be recommended by the college to **participate** in the **provincial** competition.

Betty: It's really wonderful to **propose** to work together to finish this competition and win the prize. It gave me a better understanding of the company's **operations**. **What's more**, I've learned that entrepreneurship is not a simple thing, but a big challenge.

Lucy: Entrepreneurship is not only an idea. To put it into practice, we should understand the entrepreneurial risks, write down our entrepreneurial ideas in detail, and **highlight** our innovation points to attract the attention of the judges.

Elaine: We also need to **calculate** the group cost and income in detail, and analyze the management risk, personal and property risk.

Ann: Everyone has put in their own efforts for this competition and it's really nice to work with you.

Betty: Entrepreneurship requires relevant knowledge, relevant skills, and enthusiasm for entrepreneurship. Team cooperation and communication are really important. Entrepreneurship can't be completed by only one person. It requires the cooperation of several people. Contemporary **enterprise** without a strong team is unlikely to exist.

Ann: In the following competition, we should continue to improve our innovation and entrepreneurship plan and answer the judges' questions with more confidence.

Betty, Lucy and Elaine: No problem. Let's **go for it**.

Vocabulary and notes

1. the first prize: 第一名；一等奖；得头彩

2. participate: v. to take part in something；参与；参加

3. provincial: adj. belonging to or coming from a province；省的；一级行政区的

4. propose: v. to put forward something such as an idea or suggested course of action formally or officially；建议；提议；求婚；打算

5. operation: n. the act of making something carry out its function, or controlling or managing the way it works；操作；运行；手术；运作

6. what's more: 另外

7. highlight: v. move into the foreground to make more visible or prominent；突出；强调；使显著

8. calculate: v. to work out or estimate a figure using mathematics；计算；预测；核算

9. enterprise: n. organized business activities aimed specifically at growth and profit；企业；事业；公司

10. go for it: not to stop or relax until you reach your goal；尽力争取；试一试

Activity

Make up a dialogue based on the following situation.

Suppose you are a salesman from Beijing Sunrise Foreign Trade Company, you're going to negotiate with Mr. Ryan, a sales manager from a foreign trade company, about the price of the products, the package and shipment to reach an agreement.

Section II Extensive Reading

Passage 1

On Food Innovation

The promise of finding **long-term** technological solutions to the problem of world food shortages seems difficult to fulfill. Many innovations that were once heavily supported and publicized have fallen by the **wayside**. The proposals themselves were technically feasible, but they **proved** to be economically unviable（行不通的）and to yield food products culturally unacceptable to their consumers.

One characteristic common to unsuccessful food innovations has been that, even with extensive government **support**, they often have not been technologically adapted or culturally acceptable to the people for whom they had been developed. A successful new technology, therefore, must fit the entire social cultural system in which it is to find a place. Security of crop yield, practicality of **storage**, and costs are much more significant than previously been realized by the advocates of new technologies.

The **adoption** of new food technologies depends on more than these technical and cultural considerations; economic factors and governmental policies also strongly influence the ultimate success of any innovation. Economists（经济学家）in the Anglo-American tradition have taken the lead in investigating the economics of technological innovation. Although they **exaggerate** in claiming that profitability is the key factor guiding technical change—they **completely** disregard（忽视）the substantial effects of culture—they are correct in stressing the importance of profits. Most technological innovations in agriculture can be fully used only by large landowners and are only adopted if these **profit-oriented** business people believe that the innovation will increase their incomes. Thus, innovations that carry high rewards for big **agribusiness** groups will be adopted even if they harm segments of the population and reduce the availability of food in a country. Further, should a new technology promise to alter substantially the profits and losses associated with any production system, those with economic power will strive to maintain and improve their own positions. Therefore, although technical advances in food production and processing will perhaps be needed to ensure food **availability**, meeting food needs will depend much more on equalizing economic power among the various **segments** of the populations within the developing countries themselves.

Vocabulary and notes

1. long-term: adj. relating to or affecting a time long into the future；长期的；长远的；长期有效的

2. wayside: n. the side of a road or path；路边；路旁

3. prove: v. to establish the truth or existence of something by providing evidence or argument；证明；证实；展现

4. support: n. active assistance and encouragement to, or an approving and encouraging attitude toward, somebody or something；支持；支护；支撑；支承

5. storage: n. the act of storing something, or the condition of being stored；贮存；存储（方式）

6. adoption: n. the decision to use or accept a particular idea, method, law, or attitude；（想法、计划、名字等的）采用；领养

7. exaggerate: v. to state that something is better, worse, larger, more common, or more important than is true or usual；夸大；夸张；言过其实

8. completely: adv. if something is done completely, every part of it is done；非常；完全地；彻底地

9. profit-oriented: 盈利性；以利益为导向的

10. agribusiness: n. the operations and businesses that are associated with large-scale farming；农业综合企业；农业综合经营

11. availability: n. the condition of being available, especially of being easily accessible or obtainable；有效；可得到的东西

12. segment: n. any of the parts or sections into which an object or group is divided；段；部分；片

13. One characteristic common to unsuccessful food innovations has been that, even with extensive government support, they often have not been technologically adapted or culturally acceptable to the people for whom they had been developed. 不成功的食品创新有一个共同点，即使得到政府的广泛支持，它们在技术和文化上都不能为其开发的人所接受。

14. Although they exaggerate in claiming that profitability is the key factor guiding technical change—they completely disregard the substantial effects of culture—they are correct in stressing the importance of profits. 尽管他们夸大了盈利能力是引导技术变革的关键因素，但他们完全忽视了文化的重要影响，他们强调利润的重要性是正确的。

15. Therefore, although technical advances in food production and processing will perhaps be needed to ensure food availability, meeting food needs will depend much more on equalizing economic power among the various segments of the populations within the developing countries themselves. 因此，虽然可能需要在粮食生产和加工方面取得技术进步，以确保粮食供应，但满足粮食需求将更多地取决于发展中国家内部各阶层人口之间的经济力量均衡。

 译文

论食品创新

寻找能够长期解决世界粮食短缺问题的技术这一承诺似乎很难实现。许多曾经受到大力支持和宣传的创新，后来都被搁置一边。这些提议本身在技术上是可行的，但事实证明，它们在经济上是行不通的，而且生产的食品在文化上也不为消费者所接受。

不成功的食品创新有一个共同点，即使得到政府的广泛支持，它们在技术和文化上都不能为其开发的人所接受。因此，一项成功的新技术必须与整个社会文化体系相适应。作物产量的安全性、储藏的实用性和成本比以前新技术倡导者所认识到的要重要得多。

采用新的食品技术不仅仅取决于这些技术和文化因素；经济因素和政府政策也极大地影响任何创新的最终成功。英美传统的经济学家率先研究技术创新的经济学。尽管他们夸大了盈利能力是引导技术变革的关键因素，但他们完全忽视了文化的重要影响，他们强调利润的重要性是正确的。大多数农业技术创新只有大地主才能充分利用，只有当这些以利润为导向的商人相信这种创新能增加他们的收入时，才会采用。因此，对大型农业企业集团带来高额回报的创新将被采用，即使它们损害了部分人群的利益，减少了一个国家的粮食供应。此外，如果一项新技术承诺要大幅度改变任何生产系统的盈亏，那些有经济实力的人将努力保持和改善自己的利益。因此，虽然可能需要在粮食生产和加工方面取得技术进步，以确保粮食供应，但满足粮食需求将更多地取决于发展中国家内部各阶层人口之间的经济力量均衡。

📖 Passage 2

Remarks of President Barack Obama

Weekly Address
Saturday, April 18, 2009

It's not news to say that we are living through challenging times: The worst economic **downturn** since the Great Depression. A credit crisis has made that downturn worse. And a fiscal disaster has accumulated over a period of years.

In the year 2000, we had projected **budget** surpluses in the trillions, and Washington appeared to be on the road to fiscal（财政的）**stability**. Eight years later, when I walked in the door, the projected budget deficit for this year alone was $1.3 trillion. And in order to jumpstart（启动）our struggling economy, we were forced to make investments that added to that deficit through the American Recovery and Reinvestment Act.

But as surely as our future depends on building a new energy economy, controlling health care costs and **ensuring** that our kids are once again the best educated in the world, it also depends on restoring a sense of responsibility and accountability to our federal budget. Without significant change to steer away from ever-expanding deficits and debt, we are on an **unsustainable** course.

So today, we simply cannot afford to perpetuate a system in Washington where politicians and bureaucrats（官僚主义）make decisions behind closed doors, with little accountability for the consequences; where billions are **squandered** on programs that have outlived their usefulness, or exist solely because of the power of a **lobbyist** or interest group; and where outdated technology and information systems undermine efficiency, **threaten** our security, and fail to serve an engaged citizenry.

If we're going to rebuild our economy on a solid foundation, we need to change the way we do business in Washington. We need to restore the American people's confidence in their government-that it is on their side, spending their money wisely, to meet their families' needs.

The goal is to give all Americans a voice in their government and ensure that they know exactly how we're spending their money-and can hold us accountable（负有责任的）for the results.

None of this will be easy. Big change never is. But with the leadership of these individuals, I am confident that we can break our bad habits, put an end to the mismanagement that has plagued our government, and start living within our means again. That is how we will get our deficits **under control** and move from recovery to prosperity. And that is how we will give the American people the kind of government they expect and deserve—one that is efficient, accountable and fully worthy of their trust.

Thank you.

Vocabulary and notes

1. remark: n. a few words that give the facts or your opinion about someone or something；评论；言论

2. downturn: n. a period or trend in which business or economic activity is reduced or is less successful；低迷时期；下滑

3. budget: n. a statement of the financial position of a country for the financial year, with proposals for spending and taxation, presented in a speech by the Chancellor of the Exchequer；预算；政府的年度预算

4. stability: n. the condition of being stable；稳定（性）；稳固（性）

5. ensure: v. to make sure that something will happen or be available；确保；保证

6. unsustainable: adj. not capable of continuing at the same rate or level；不能持续的；无法维持的

7. squander: v. to spend or use something precious in a wasteful and extravagant way；浪费；挥霍

8. lobbyist: n. someone who lobbies politicians or other people in authority, also lobbyer；说客；游说者

9. threaten: v. to express or indicate an intention to harm or kill somebody；威胁；危及；恐吓

10. under control: in or into a state of being successfully controlled；处于控制之下；在控制中

11. And in order to jumpstart our struggling economy, we were forced to make investments that added to that deficit through the American Recovery and Reinvestment Act. 为了启动我们举步维艰的经济，我们被迫通过《美国复苏与再投资决案》进行投资，这进一步增加了赤字。

12. We need to restore the American people's confidence in their government—that it is on their side, spending their money wisely, to meet their families' needs. 我们需要恢复美国人民对政府的信心——政府站在他们一边，明智地花钱，满足他们家庭的需要。

13. That is how we will get our deficits under control and move from recovery to prosperity. And that is how we will give the American people the kind of government they expect and deserve—one that is efficient, accountable and fully worthy of their trust. 这就是我们如何控制赤字，从复苏走向繁荣的途径。这就是我们将如何给美国人民一个他们期望和应得的政府——一个高效、负责任和完全值得他们信任的政府。

 译文

奥巴马总统的讲话

每周演讲

2009年4月18日，星期六

我们正经历一个充满挑战的时代：大萧条以来最严重的经济衰退，这并不是什么新闻。一场信贷危机使得经济下滑更加严重。一场财政灾难也已积蓄数年之久。

在2000年，我们曾预计有数万亿的预算盈余，而华盛顿似乎正走向财政稳定的道路。八年后，当我入主白宫时，仅今年一年的预算赤字就达1.3万亿美元。为了启动我们举步维艰的经济，我们被迫通过《美国复苏与再投资法案》进行投资，这进一步增加了赤字。

但是，正如我们的未来取决于建立一个新的能源经济，控制医疗保健费用，确保我们的孩子再次受到世界上最好的教育一样，这也取决于重拾我们对联邦预算的责任感。如果不做出重大改变，避免不断扩大的赤字和债务，我们就走上了不可持续的道路。

因此，今天，我们根本无法承受这样一种体制：政客和官僚们闭门决策，对后果几乎不负责任；数十亿美元被浪费在那些已经失去效用的项目上，或者仅仅因为说客或利益集团的力量而存在的项目；过时的技术和信息系统破坏了效率，威胁着我们的安全，无法为相关的市民服务。

如果我们要在坚实的基础上重建我们的经济，我们需要改变我们在华盛顿的行事方式。我们需要恢复美国人民对政府的信心——政府站在他们一边，明智地花钱，满足他们家庭的需要。

我们的目标是让所有美国人在他们的政府中有发言权，并确保他们确切知道我们是如何花钱的，并能让我们对结果负责。

　　这一切都不容易。大变革从来都不是这么简单的。但在美国人民的领导下，我相信我们能够改掉我们的坏习惯，结束困扰我们政府的管理不善的问题，开始量入为出。这就是我们如何控制赤字，从复苏走向繁荣的途径。这就是我们将如何给美国人民一个他们期望和应得的政府——一个高效、负责任和完全值得他们信任的政府。

　　谢谢。

Section III *Case Analysis in Intercultural Communication*

Sending Gifts

As a foreign student at the University of Wisconsin in Madison, Keiko Ihara (Japanese) was on a strict budget. She had all her tuition and books paid for by scholarships and grants and until recently was comfortably housed in the dormitory. Wanting to live in the community rather than in the dormitory, she found a small apartment to share with a friend. Her college friends, knowing of her situation, offered to round up some of the necessary items for apartment living. Keiko politely declined, saying she could manage. Wanting to help out her friends she found some old but still usable household appliances and furniture. Mary had an old desk that was in her garage. Ed had chairs from his uncle, and Joe and Marion had a few extra dishes. They cheerfully brought them over one day. Keiko seemed very embarrassed, but gracefully accepted them, sincerely and profusely thanked them. The following week they were each presented with a gift from Keiko. Mary got an ornate jewelry box, Ed a volume of woodcuts by a famous Japanese artist, and Joe and Marion a beautiful Japanese vase, all of which were of considerable worth and value, much more than the old things they had donated to her. They all protested that she could not afford to give such elaborate gifts; They really expected nothing as the household items were not really being used and they would rather have her to use them. Keiko, however, insisted that they take the gifts. In the end, they accepted the gifts, although they all felt uncomfortable as they knew she was really sacrificing to give them.

Questions for discussion

1. What do you think of Keiko insisting on giving valuable gifts to her college friends?
2. Why did Keiko's friends feel very uncomfortable when they received valuable gifts in return?

分析：庆子坚持给她的大学朋友送贵重的礼物，因为在日本这样的国家，交换礼物是根深蒂固的社会传统。如果你收到一份礼物，却没有礼物作为回报，你很可能会制造交往危机。如果交往危机严重，一个不提供礼物作为回报的人可能会被认为是粗鲁或不礼貌的。因此，在日本，礼物是一种象征性的方式，表示赞赏、尊重、感激和进一步的关系。

玛丽、埃德和马里恩将这些二手物品作为礼物送给庆子，庆子却不了解美国人经常把他们用过的家居用品捐给教堂、社区或赠送给朋友。在庆子的文化中，没有把用过的家居用品当作礼物送给朋友的习俗，作为回报，庆子花钱购买了新的物品，所以当她的朋友们收到贵重的礼物作为回报时，感到非常不自在。

Section Ⅳ Practical Writing: Post

海报这一名称，最早起源于上海，是一种宣传方式。旧时，海报是用于戏剧、电影等演出，活动的招帖。

海报一般由标题、正文和落款三部分组成。

1. 标题

海报的标题写法较多，可单独在第一行中间写上"海报"字样；可直接用活动的内容做题目，如"舞讯""影讯""球讯"等；也可用一些描述性的文字，如"××再×显风采"。

2. 正文

海报的正文部分要用简洁的文字写清楚活动的目的和意义，活动的主要项目、时间、地点等，参加的具体方法及一些必要的注意事项等。

3. 落款

海报要求署上主办单位的名称及海报的发文日期。

Sample

你校学生会组织了英语夏令营活动以便同学们学好英语、建立良好的人际关系，每年暑假有形式多样的活动（如学习英文歌曲、舞蹈、游戏等），活动费用比较低。请你用英语写一张海报向同学们介绍一下夏令营的情况并邀请同学们参加夏令营活动。

词数：120~150词。

分析：

文体信息

题目要求用英语写一张海报。海报属于应用文，它是一种带有装饰的宣传广告，内容以多是大众喜闻乐见的消息为主，如影讯、展览、演出信息、友谊赛等。为了尽可能使更多的人知道，海报是贴在人来人往而且非常醒目的地方，有时还配以绘画图案以吸引观众。

写作关键

（1）作文时表达要符合海报的特点，开门见山，直奔主题。

（2）正确使用人称、时态和语态，文中应该用第三人称，邀请性的语句用第二人称；时态为现在时态，多为一般现在时。

（3）海报一定要具体真实地写明活动的地点、时间及主要内容。

（4）注意海报的语言特征。文中可以用些鼓动性的词语，但不可夸大实事；海报文字要求简洁明了，篇幅要简洁明了。

Sample

English Summer Camp[①]

Would you like to spend the summer vacation with your friends?[②] Are you eager to practice your English and get your spoken English improved while enjoying yourself? Come on! Join us in the English Summer Camp.

The Summer Camp is devoted to[③] the improvement of its members English as well as the establishment of good interpersonal relationships. Every summer, there are a wide variety of[④] activities, such as English songs learning, dance training and games. The members can learn a lot in a relaxed atmosphere. In this way, not only do the members improve their English[⑤], they also learn how to get along well with others. In addition,[⑥] the membership fee is low. Don't hesitate any longer—join us and enjoy your summer vacation.[⑦]

School Student Union

June 7, 2010[⑧]

分析：

（1）海报标题恰如其分，宣传夏令营。

（2）正文开头灵活使用问句使海报内容显得不呆板，同时又能起到渲染的作用。

（3）be devoted to 高级词汇，增加作文亮点。

（4）a wide variety of "各式各样的"，表明作者的语言功底。

（5）倒装句，文章句式多。

（6）in addition "另外，此外"，上下文连接好。

（7）祈使句，丰富文章句式，发出邀请，希望大家参加活动

（8）结尾符合海报格式。

Practice

白山宾馆新开业，为吸引宾客，希望在互联网上进行宣传。请你用英语为其写一篇海报。主要内容包括：

（1）地点：距白山入口处500米。

（2）房间及价格：单人间（共20间），100元/天；双人间（共15间），150元/天；热水淋浴。

（3）餐饮：餐厅（中、西餐），咖啡厅（茶、咖啡）。

（4）游泳池：全天免费开放。

（5）欢迎预定。

注意：词数120左右，开头语已为你写好。

Practice

Welcome to Baishan Mountain Hotel!

Section V Grammar: Sentences Constituents & Main Structures（句子成分及主要句型结构）

一、句子成分

句子成分包括主语、谓语、表语、宾语、同位语、定语、状语和补足语等。主语和谓语是句子的主体部分，表语、宾语、定语、状语、补足语和同位语等是句子的次要部分

* 主语说明谓语所表示的动作或状态的执行者。名词（短语）、代词、数词、不定式（短语）、动名词（短语）和从句等皆可作主语。

例：Nobody can help you. 没人能帮你。（代词作主语）

例：I can help you. 我能够帮助你。

例：Travelling abroad is popular these years. 近年来出国旅游很流行。（动名词短语作主语）

* 谓语用来描述主语的行为动作或所处的状态。谓语的中心词是限定动词，有人称、数和时态的变化。

例：Lily worked for the company for three years. 莉莉为这家公司工作了三年。

例：The old man must be sent to hospital at once. 这个老人必须马上送医院。

* 表语与前面的系动词一起，用来说明主语的特征、类属、状态、身份等。充当表语的可以是单词、短语或从句。

例：Mary often looks cheerful. 玛丽看上去总是很高兴。（形容词作表语）

例：Anna is Canadian. 安娜是加拿大人。（名词作表语）

例：My hobby is growing flowers. 我的爱好是种花。（动名词短语作表语）

* 宾语表示动作的对象或承受者，一般位于及物动词和介词后面。

宾语有单宾语、双宾语、复合宾语等。双宾语又分为直接宾语和间接宾语。直接宾语表示动作的直接承受者或结果，大多数动词后跟直接宾语。

例：We love peace. 我们热爱和平。

间接宾语表示动作是对谁的或为谁做的。

例：Auntie gave her a toy car. 姑姑给我一个玩具汽车。（her 为间接宾语，a toy car 为直接宾语）

"宾语+宾语补足语"构成了复合宾语，宾语与补足语之间具有逻辑上的主谓关系。

例：We all find Tom a nice boy. 我们都发现汤姆是一个不错的男孩。（Tom 为宾语，a nice boy 为宾语补足语）

宾语可以由名词（短语）、代词、数词、名词化的形容词、不定式（短语）、动名词

Credit, like a looking-glass, broken once, is gone. 信誉像镜子，破碎无法补。

（短语）、从句等充当。

例：May I see your tickets please? 我看一下你的票好吗？（名词作宾语）

例：Where did you buy it? 你在哪儿买的它？（代词作宾语）

* 同位语是对前面句子中某一成分作进一步解释、说明，与前面名词在语法上处于同等地位。同位语常常置于被说明的词之后，可以作同位语的有名词、代词、数词和从句等。

例：I have two foreign friends, a Canadian and an American. 我有两个外籍朋友，一个是加拿大人，一个是美国人。（名词作同位语）

例：Are you five ready to read books? 你们五个都准备好阅读了吗？（数词作同位语）

* 定语是用来描述名词或代词的修饰语，它常放在名词前后构成名词短语。定语可分为前置定语和后置定语两种。

（1）前置定语。可以充当前置定语的有形容词、代词、数词、名词、名词所有格、动词的 -ing 形式、动词的 -ed 形式等。

例：It is a difficult problem. 这是一个棘手的问题。（形容词作前置定语）

例：This is a stone table. 这是一张石桌。（名词作前置定语）

例：Put the child in the sleeping bag. 把孩子放进睡袋。（动名词作前置定语）

（2）后置定语。可以充当后置定语的有形容词、副词、介词短语、不定式（短语）、动词的 -ing 形式、动词的 -ed 形式、从句等。

例：I have got something interesting to tell you. 我有很有趣的事情要告诉你。（形容词作后置定语）

例：He lost his new pen (that was) bought last week. 他把上周刚买的新钢笔弄丢了。（定语从句作后置定语，也可缩写为分词短语）

* 状语是用来修饰动词、形容词、副词或句子的一种成分。它可以表示时间、地点、方式、比较、程度、原因、目的、结果、条件和让步等。充当状语的有副词、介词短语、不定式、动词的 –ing 形式、动词的 –ed 形式、形容词和名词等。

例：To get a good view, he climbed to the top of the hill. 为了能看得清楚，他爬到了山顶上。（不定式作状语）

例：Tom speaks English very fast. 汤姆说英语很快。（副词作状语）

例：Don't step on the grass. 请勿踩踏草地。（介词短语作状语）

* 补语是用来说明宾语或主语的性质、状态等的一种句子成分。名词、形容词、副词、介词短语、现在分词、过去分词、不定式等皆可作补足语。含有宾语补足语的句子在变为被动句时，宾语补足语便成了主语补足语。

例：She was elected chairman of the company. 她当选为公司主席。（名词作主语补足语）

例：We all find him nice. 我们都认为他很好。（形容词作宾语补足语）

二、基本句型结构

英语中最基本的句型有五种。其他各种句型都是由这五种基本句型转换来的。

汉语名称	英语简称
主语+谓语	S+V
主语+谓语+宾语	S+V+O
主语+系动词+表语	S+V+O
主语+谓语+间接宾语+直接宾语	S+V+Oi+Od
主语+谓语+宾语+宾语补足语	S+V+O+C

例：She never lies. 她从不撒谎。

例：He has accepted our invitation. 他已经接受了我们的邀请。

例：The weather is warm. 天气很暖和。

例：She gave me a book. 她给我一本书。

例：We all call the baby Jane. 我们都叫这个婴儿简。

最后一种需要提到的就是 there be 句型（存在句）哪儿……有……

例：There are four students studying English in the room. 房间里有四位同学正在学习英语。

三、句子种类

英语句子按照使用目的和交际功能分为陈述句、疑问句、祈使句、感叹句；按照结构分为简单句、并列句和复合句。

例：I know he will come. 我知道你会来的。

例：Be sure to come on time. 请务必按时来。

例：Let's have a rest. 咱们休息一会。（包括说话者）

例：Let us try again. 让我们再试一次。（不包括说话者）

例：Are your parents doctors? 你父母是医生吗？

例：When shall we start the new plan? 我们什么时候启动新计划？

例：Give me a hand, will you? 帮我一把，好吗？

例：What a wonderful plan! 多么棒的计划！

例：How wonderful a plan! 多么棒的计划！

Exercise 1: Sentences Constituents and Main Structures（句子成分及主要句型结构）

一、指出下列句子中主语的中心词

1. The elegant lady over there is my English teacher. (   )

2. The doctor with two nurses is walking into the ward. (   )

3. There is an old man walking toward me. (   )

4. This beautiful English-Chinese dictionary was given by my sister last year. (   )

5. Lucy, along with Tom, is watering the plants in the field. (   )

二、指出下列句子中谓语的中心词

1. She don't like the photos on the wall. (   )

2. There will be an important meeting in the conference room tomorrow morning. (   )

3. Did Tom have bread and milk for his breakfast? (   )

4. What I want to say to you is this. (   )

5. Whom did you give my money to? (   )

三、指出下列句子中的宾语

1. My sister hasn't finished his homework yet. (   )

2. Open your mouth please! (   )

3. Most people in China can speak English. (   )

4. You should focus on your pronunciation. (   )

5. How many new words did you learn last class? (   )

四、指出下列句子中的定语

1. May I know your family name? (   )

2. The man downstairs is playing piano. (   )

3. I have something important to tell you. (   )

4. This long story is really boring. (   )

5. Can you pass me the third bottle? (   )

五、指出下列句子中的状语

1. She heard the noise next door every night. (   )

2. Many young people like to playing games at home. (   )

3. We began to learn English when we were ten years old. (   )

4. If it rains tomorrow, I won't go to the library. (   )

5. She loves the parks because she loves breathing the fresh air. (   )

六、指出下列句子中的宾语补足语

1. I found it really difficult to finish the task. (   )

2. My father had his car repaired yesterday. (   )

3. We call him Tom all the time. (   )

4. We saw her climb the stairs. (   )

5. I hear the boy crying angrily. (   )

七、判断下列句子的基本句型

1. The sun rises. (   )

2. The cake tastes sweet. (   )

3. I will give you ten dollars. (   )

4. What they did doesn't matter. (   )

5. My mother enjoys cooking. (   )

6. I want to eat a piece of cake. (   )

7. She felt a little bit tired. (   )

8. My parents bought me a bike. (   )

9. I want to have my hair cut. (   )

10. Tom's grandmother always tells him interesting stories. (   )

11. She is making coffee. (   )

12. Her face turned pale. (   )

13. They find the classroom empty. (   )

14. I have nothing to do. (   )

15. She lent me a book. (   )

16. My mother told me not to play on the street. (   )

17. Her dream is to be a teacher. (   )

18. They call me Peter. (   )

19. They danced for nearly an hour. (   )

20. He keeps silent all the time. (   )

八、单项选择

1. I help her _____ she helps me.

  A. but   B. and   C. yet   D. or

2. Hurry up, _____ you'll be late for the meeting.

A. or   B. and   C. yet   D. so

3. Not only is she my teacher, _____ she is my friend.

A. also   B. too   C. but   D. and

4. She apologized, _____ I forgave her.

A. so   B. but   C. yet   D. or

5. Work hard, _____ you'll fail the exam.

A. otherwise   B. but   C. so   D. therefore

6. There _____ an apple and five oranges in the bag.

A. are   B. is   C. were   D. be

7. There _____ some milk, some candies and several apples on the table.

A. is   B. are   C. has   D. have

8. There _____ anything interesting in today's TV program.

A. isn't   B. are   C. is   D. aren't

9. There _____ many elephants in Africa.

A. is   B. has   C. are   D. have

10. Are there any _____ on the table?

A. pork   B. cheese   C. tomatoes   D. paper

九、翻译

1. 太阳落山了。

2. 我借给汤姆10元。

3. 我妹妹正在画画。

4. 这药太苦了。

5. 这款裙子卖的很好。

6. 我听到她们在隔壁唱歌。

7. 露西不喜欢外出。

8. 锻炼身体非常重要。

9. 老师叫我们不要在教室里大声说话。

10. 我想去修我的自行车。

11. 我长胖了。

12. 中国变得越来越强大了。

13. 努力可以改变人们的命运。

14. 情绪可以影响人们的身心健康。

15. 诚实是重要的品质。

16. 我希望你能理解。

17. 我正在给她看我的照片。

18. 你不应该轻易放弃。

19. 她拥抱了她的母亲。

20. 世界需要和平。

扫一扫查看
练习参考答案

扫一扫查看
本章拓展资料

Unit 6

Entrepreneurship

扫一扫查看
本章教学PPT

Learning Objectives

【About Knowledge】

1. To understand the meaning of entrepreneurship.

2. To master useful words and expressions.

3. To talk about starting your own business.

To know more about Noun Clause.

【About Skills】

To know more about writing a notice.

Section 1 *Dialogues*

Dialogue 1

Starting Your Own Business

David is having a conversation with his fellow classmate, Tom, about their future career.

David: **Nowadays**, with the competition in the job market becoming increasingly fierce for college **graduates**, some ambitious students have done their utmost to start their own businesses and make it even during college.

Tom: Yeah, that's it. Over the years, there have been many successful cases of this **phe-**

nomenon and I think such attempts should be encouraged and promoted by both the universities and society.

David: You know, starting the business always has a risk during its process. Do you have any advice on it?

Tom: Of course. I think the most important one is that when you **face with** unknown challenges, you should be **audacious** enough to embark on a perilous journey while most of your peers enjoy stable salaries.

David: And I think even if you fail, you can't be beaten down. You should keep exploring for new opportunities and work tirelessly until you succeed. If you really want to get success, you should have a positive attitude, cultivate your **creativity** and innovation ability.

Tom: Yeah, you are right. So, you want to **start your business** at the right time, don't you?

David: I would like a stable work and get a normal **salary** when I graduate from university. But I have heard that you want to do some business and you have experience in doing it, is it right?

Tom: Yeah, **at the beginning**, I sold some daily commodities such as pens, wash basins, clothes hangers and so on. Then I sold old books which are from senior students to underclassmen.

David: Oh, you are so **creative**, and I hope you can achieve success in the near future.

Tom: Thank you!

Vocabulary and notes

1. nowadays: adv. in the present, or in the times in which we are now living, usually in contrast to the past；现在；现今；目前

2. graduate: n. somebody who has obtained a diploma or degree, e.g. from a high school or college；毕业生；大学毕业生

3. phenomenon: n. something that happens or exists in society, or nature, especially something that is studied because it is difficult to under stand；现象；杰出的人

4. face with: v. 面临

5. audacious: adj. bold, daring, or fearless, especially in challenging assumptions or conventions；敢于冒险的；大胆的

6. creativity: n. the ability to use the imagination to develop new and original ideas or

things, especially in an artistic context；创造力；艺术创新

7. start your business: 创业

8. salary: n. a fixed annual sum, paid at regular intervals, usually monthly, to an employee, especially for professional or clerical work；薪金

9. at the beginning: 在当初；首先

10. creative: adj. involving a lot of imagination and new ideas 创造的；有创新性的

Dialogue 2

Job Seeking

Susan is having a conversation with her fellow classmate, David, about their future career.

Susan: Why don't you start searching for a job? Our classmates have been on the job-hunting journey.

David: I want something more **challenging**.

Susan: Like what?

David: To run my own business and be my own boss.

Susan: Why do you want to start your own business? Students of your **major** can easily land a job nowadays.

David: Well, I hate being controlled by others, and I don't want to start **at the bottom of** a **steep** corporate ladder.

Susan: I don't mean to **discourage** you, but do you know that most new business fail? Are you fully prepared?

David: Sure, I am. To avoid risks, I'll start by opening a small online store in order to make the first **bucket** of gold of my life.

Susan: That's down-to-earth. The profits may be low, but you don't have to put in too much **overhead**.

David: Yeah, I can work at home, **saving** the cost of renting an office. And I don't have to **hire** an extra hand unless I'm extremely busy.

Susan: Good! In that way, little by little, you can accumulate enough start-up investment for your own company.

Vocabulary and notes

1. challenging: adj. difficult in an interesting way that tests your ability；挑战性的；考验能力的；挑起争论的

2. major: n. the field of study in which a college or university student chooses to specialize；专业课；主修课程

3. at the bottom of: 在……的底部

4. steep: adj. sloping very sharply, often to the extent of being almost vertical；陡的；陡峭的；突然的；急剧的

5. discourage: v. to tend to prevent something from happening by making it more difficult or unpleasant；阻止；劝阻；阻拦；使灰心

6. bucket: n. a container, usually cylindrical in shape with an open top and a semicircular handle, used for catching or holding liquids or solids；吊桶；大量

7. overhead: n. the general recurring costs of running a business, excluding the costs of labour and materials, e.g. rent, maintenance, and utilities；企业一般管理费用

8. save: v. to reduce or limit the expense of something；节省；节约

9. hire: v. to employ somebody to work for you, or pay somebody to do a job for you；雇用；聘用；租用；录用

Dialogue 3

Finding a Job

Jean is having a conversation with his friend, Stephen, about their future career.

Jean: Why is it so hard to find a good job and pursue the career I want?

Stephen: I don't know! You tell me! What is it that you want to do?

Jean: I want a good job as a manager that **pays** well and is interesting at the same time.

Stephen: But, a manager of what? It sounds as though you have not thought this through very well.

Jean: What do you mean? I've been thinking about it **ever since** I got into university.

Stephen: Aha! That's the problem. You have been "considering", but do you have a "plan"? How are you going to **achieve** it?

Jean: Yes. I've written my resume and I've been to several of those job seminars.

Stephen: So, what sort of work are you interested in? What are you majoring in at university?

Jean: I'm doing Commerce and want to get into marketing.

Stephen: OK. What sort of **marketing** do you want to get into?

Jean: I don't know. Anything that pays well!

Stephen: Well, I think there is something wrong with your attitude towards **choosing** a career. When choosing a career, you first need to be clear. The important thing is where your work interests is, and the remuneration should be the last **consideration** for you.

Jean: But, it's important that I get well paid for the work I do.

Stephen: Hey! **Hang on a minute**. The first thing you have to figure out is which part of marketing you like to do. Second, you must understand that you will start from the most basic work in the future.

Jean: But I'm an undergraduate degree. I shouldn't have to start at the bottom.

Stephen: I'm afraid you don't like to hear this, but you have to know that your **degree** is just like a ticket, and it just allows you to enter the gate.

Jean: How much more do I need? If I get a good degree, why isn't it enough?

Stephen: How many people do you think are going to apply for the job you want?

Jean: Well, a lots , I suppose.

Stephen: So, have you really thought it through? Have you made a list of your **strengths** and weaknesses? Have you worked out how you are going to sell your abilities?

Jean: No. Not really.

Stephen: Well, believe me. That's the core of the game. Sell your ideas, sell your ability, convince someone you are the best choice for the job; That's what selling's all about.

Vocabulary and notes

1. pay: v. to give somebody money for work done or for goods or services provided；付费；偿还；交纳；付酬

2. ever since: during the whole period of time since something happened；从……以来

3. achieve: v. to succeed in doing or gaining something, usually with effort；完成；（凭长期努力）达到（某目标、地位、标准）；成功

4. marketing: n. the business activity of presenting products or services in such a way as to

make them desirable；营销；促销；销售活动

5. choose: v. to decide which of a number of different things or people is best or most appropriate；选择；选取；挑选；决定

6. consideration: n. thoughtful concern for or sensitivity toward the feelings of others；顾及；报酬；斟酌；仔细考虑

7. Hang on a minute: I used when you are annoyed and want someone to stop what they are doing and listen；等一下；等一会儿

8. degree: n. the relative extent, amount, intensity, or level of something, especially when compared with other things；度；程度；度数（温度单位）；（大学）学位

9. strength: n. a quality or an ability that a person or thing has that gives them an advantage；优势；实力；力气

Dialogue 4

Job Seeking

Ryan is having a conversation with his fellow classmate, John, about their future career.

Ryan: Hey, buddy, how's your **job-seeking** going?

John: Don't mention it. Everything is **in a mess**.

Ryan: Doesn't **sound** good.

John: Well, what about you? I heard that you were preparing to **set up** a **college** club, is that true?

Ryan: Yeah. Now, I am applying for a bank **loan**.

John: Wow! It must be exciting and challenging.

Ryan: Do you want to join us?

John: Me?

Ryan: Exactly! I think you are a **genius** in IT.

John: But what can I do in your club?

Ryan: You know. The Internet has become an important approach in doing business. So, you can **take charge of** establishing our website and overseeing its operation.

John: Are you serious? That's the very job I'm looking for.

Ryan: Great! Let's do it together and fight for our promising future.

Do as the Romans do (or Do as they do at Rome). 入乡随俗。

Vocabulary and notes

1. job-seeking: 求职；找工作

2. in a mess: a situation in which there are a lot of problems and difficulties；肮脏；混乱；困难

3. sound: v. to give a particular impression about a physical or mental condition via speech or writing；响；听起来……的；鸣警报；拉响警报

4. set up: to establish something, or bring something into being；建立；创立；发起；开办

5. college: n. an institution of higher learning that provides education to undergraduates and awards bachelor's and sometimes master's degrees；学院；大学；大专

6. loan: n. an amount of money that a person, business, or country borrows, especially from a bank；贷款；借款；借用

7. genius: n. somebody with exceptional ability, especially somebody whose intellectual or creative achievements gain worldwide recognition；天才；天赋；天才人物；天资

8. take charge of: nu. 主管；负责

Activity

Make up a dialogue based on the following situation.

Suppose that you are going to start your own business, now you want to share this idea with your roommate and wish to get some suggestion from him or her.

Section II Extensive Reading

 Passage 1

Successful Entrepreneurship

It is well that young men should begin at the beginning and **occupy** the most subordinate positions. Many of the leading businessmen of Pittsburgh had a serious responsibility thrust upon them at the very threshold of their career. They were introduced to the broom, and spent the first hours of their business lives sweeping out the office. I notice we have **janitors** and janitresses（女工友）now in offices, and our young men unfortunately miss that salutary（有利的）

branch of business education. But if **by chance** the professional sweeper is absent any morning, the boy who has the genius of the future partner in him will not hesitate to try his hand at the broom. It does not hurt the newest comer to **sweep out** the office if necessary. I was one of those sweepers myself.

Assuming that you have all obtained employment and fairly started, my advice to you is "aim high". I would not give a fig for the young man who does not already see himself the partner or the head of an important firm. Do not rest contently for a moment in your thoughts as head clerk, or foreman, or general manager **in any concern**, no matter which position you are in. Say to yourself, "My place is at the top." Be king in your dreams.

And here is the prime（主要的）condition of success, the great secret: concentrate（专注于）your energy, thought, and capital exclusively upon the business in which you are **engaged**. Having begun in one line, resolve to fight it out on that line, to lead in it, adopt every improvement, have the best machinery, and know the most about it.

The companies which fail are those which have **scattered** their capital, which means that they have scattered their brains. They have investments（投资）in this, or that, or the other, here and there. "Don't put all your eggs in one basket" is all wrong. I tell you to "put all your eggs in one basket, and then watch that basket." Look round and you take notice, men who do that don't often fail. It is easy to watch and carry one basket. It is trying to carry too many baskets that breaks most eggs in this country. He who carries three baskets must put one on his head, which is apt to **tumble** and trip him up. One **fault** of the American businessman is lack of concentration.

To summarize what I have said: Aim for the highest; Never enter a bar room; Do not touch **liquor**, or if at all only at meals; Never speculate; Never live beyond your means; Make the firm's interest yours; Break orders to save owners; Concentrate; Put all your eggs in one basket, and watch that basket; Expenditure always within revenue; Lastly, be not impatient, for as Emerson says, "no one can cheat you out of ultimate success but yourselves."

Vocabulary and notes

1. occupy: v. to live in or be the established user of a place such as a home or office；占据；占领；侵占；使用

2. janitor: n. somebody whose job is to look after the cleaning and maintenance of a build-

ing, especially a school or an apartment building；看门人；照管一座房屋或办公室的工人

3. by chance: unexpectedly or without plan；偶然

4. sweep out: v. 扫掉；清除

5. assume: v. to accept that something is true without checking or confirming it；假设；假定；认为；假装

6. in any concern: 任何关注

7. engage: v. to involve somebody in an activity, or become involved or take part in an activity；从事；订婚；聘用；吸引住（注意力、兴趣）

8. scatter: v. to throw things around so that they land with an irregular distribution over a relatively wide area；撒；四散；驱散；撒播

9. tumble: v. if someone tumbles, they fall to the ground；跌倒；摔倒；倒塌；绊倒

10. fault: n. something that detracts from the integrity, functioning, or perfection of something else；故障；过错；过失；缺陷

11. liquor: n. an alcoholic drink, especially of the type produced by distillation, e.g. whiskey, rather than of the type produced by fermentation, e.g. wine or beer；酒；含酒精饮料；白酒；汤；（药学）溶液

12. It is well that young men should begin at the beginning and occupy the most subordinate positions. Many of the leading businessmen of Pittsburgh had a serious responsibility thrust upon them at the very threshold of their career. 年轻人创业之初，应该从最底层干起，这是件好事。匹兹堡的许多主要商人在他们职业生涯的开始阶段就肩负着沉重的责任。

13. I would not give a fig for the young man who does not already see himself the partner or the head of an important firm. 一个年轻人，如果不把自己想象成大公司未来的老板或者是合伙人，那我会对他不屑一顾。

14. And here is the prime condition of success, the great secret: concentrate your energy, thought, and capital exclusively upon the business in which you are engaged. Having begun in one line, resolve to fight it out on that line, to lead in it, adopt every improvement, have the best machinery, and know the most about it. 成功的首要条件和最大秘诀就是：把你的精力，思想和资本全都集中在你正从事的事业上。一旦开始从事某种职业，就要下定决心在那一领域闯出一片天地来；做这一行的领导人物，采纳每一项改进的建议，采用最优良的设备，对专业知识熟稔于心。

15. It is trying to carry too many baskets that breaks most eggs in this country. He who carries three baskets must put one on his head, which is apt to tumble and trip him up. One fault of the American businessman is lack of concentration. 人们总是试图提很多篮子，所以才打破这个国家的大部分鸡蛋。提三个篮子的人，必须把一个顶在头上，而这个篮子很可能掉下来，把他自己绊倒。美国商人的一个缺点就是不够专注。

译文

成功创业

年轻人创业之初，应该从最底层干起，这是件好事。匹兹堡的许多主要商人在他们职业生涯的开始阶段就肩负着沉重的责任。他们以扫帚相伴，以打扫办公室的方式度过了他们商业生涯的最初阶段。我注意到我们现在办公室里都有工友，于是年轻人就不幸错过了商业教育中这个有益的环节。碰巧哪天上午专职扫地的工友没有来，某个具有合伙人气质的年轻人会毫不犹豫地试着拿起扫帚。在必要时，新来的员工扫扫地也无妨，不会因此而有什么损失。我自己就扫过地。

假如你已经被录用，并且有了一个良好的开端，我对你的建议是：要志存高远。一个年轻人，如果不把自己想象成大公司未来的老板或者是合伙人，那我会对他不屑一顾。不论职位有多高，你的内心都不要满足于做一个总管、领班或者总经理。要对自己说：我要迈向顶尖！要做就做梦想中的国王！

成功的首要条件和最大秘诀就是：把你的精力、思想和资本全都集中在你正从事的事业上。一旦开始从事某种职业，就要下定决心在那一领域闯出一片天地来；做这一行的领导人物，采纳每一项改进的建议，采用最优良的设备，对专业知识熟稔于心。

一些公司的失败就在于他们分散了资金，因为这就意味着分散了他们的精力。他们投资这个，又投资那个；在这里投资，在那里投资，到处都投资。"不要把所有的鸡蛋放在一个篮子里"的说法大错特错。我要对你说："把所有的鸡蛋都放在一个篮子里，然后小心地看好那个篮子。"看看你周围，你会注意到：这么做的人很少失败。看管和携带一个篮子并不太难。人们总是试图提很多篮子，所以才打破这个国家的大部分鸡蛋。提三个篮子的人，必须把一个顶在头上，而这个篮子很可能掉下来，把他自己绊倒。美国商人的一个缺点就是不够专注。

把我的话归纳一下：要志存高远；不要出入酒吧，要滴酒不沾，或要喝也只在用餐时喝少许；不要做投机买卖；不要寅吃卯粮；要把公司的利益当作自己的利益；取消订货的目的是为了挽救货主；要专注；要把所有的鸡蛋放在一个篮子里，然后小心地看好它；要量入为出；最后，要有耐心，正如爱默生所言，"谁都无法阻止你成功，除非你自己承认自己失败。"

📖 Passage 2

Hou shuyuan: Post-90s-famale postgraduates built a bicycle station, generating one millon yuan in revenue a year

A beautiful-looking girl born in the 90s who looks delicate and fragile has become **obsessed** with outdoor cycling, which is physically demanding, and has turned this hobby into a career in Hainan. Hou Shuyuan, a second-year graduate student of Chongqing Technology and Business University, **started from scratch** and established the "517 Cycling Station". Today, the station is widely praised by cyclists, with an annual **turnover** of more than 600,000 yuan.

"I feel at home" "The last time I ride in college" "Go now" "Farewell to the smog, come to Hainan for cycling" ... In the station, there are messages from riders everywhere, and now the station has become a paradise for riders.

In the past two years since the establishment of the post, the popularity of the post has been **continuously** increasing. Since June 2013, hotel owners of Wenchang, Boao, and Xinglong have come to their door and become the franchise store of 517 Cycling Station.

"Last year we had nearly 1 million yuan in income, with a net income of more than 500,000 yuan. Now the station has set up the east line of the round-the-island cycling **route**. It is expected that in five years we will open 5 to 10 more on the central and western lines of the round-the-island cycling route. At the inn, riders will enjoy our one-stop service at that time." Hou Shuyuan said.

Speaking of New Year's **resolutions**, Hou Shuyuan stated that the next step would be to open 5 to 10 inns on the central and western routes of cycling around the island. By then, riders will be able to enjoy more convenient services. At the same time, they are discussing cooperation with travel agencies to **launch** cycling tourist special lines, etc.

Now that the school has started, Hou Shuyuan must not only run a good post, but also strengthen her studies. She feels that she cannot afford to lose her studies while starting a business.

Hou Shuyuan is convinced that the "517 Cycling Station" will definitely make use of the building of an international tourist island, and business will get better and better.

（来源：https://www.360kuai.com/pc/）

Vocabulary and notes

1. obsessed: adj. having or showing excessive or compulsive concern with something；着迷的

2. start from scratch: 从头开始；白手起家；从起跑线开始

3. turnover: n. the volume measured in dollars；[贸易] 营业额

4. continuously: adv. at every point; with unflagging resolve；连续不断地

5. route: n. an open way (generally public) for travel or transportation；路线，航线；道路，公路

6. resolution: n. a decision to do something or to behave in a certain manner；决议；决心

7. launch: v. set up or found; begin with vigor；发起，发动

8. Since June 2013, hotel owners of Wenchang, Boao, and Xinglong have come to their door and become the franchise store of 517 Cycling Station. 2013 年 6 月至今，已经有文昌、博鳌、兴隆 3 家旅店老板主动找上门来，成为 517 骑行驿站加盟店。

9. Speaking of New Year's resolutions, Hou Shuyuan stated that the next step would be to open 5 to 10 inns on the central and western routes of cycling around the island. 说到新年打算，侯姝媛表示下一步将在环岛骑行的中线和西线开 5 至 10 家驿站。

译文

侯姝媛：90 后女研究生建自行车驿站，一年骑出百万元

一位长相清秀，看起来娇娇弱弱的 90 后女孩儿，却迷上了对体力要求较高的户外骑行，并在海南将这一爱好变成了事业。重庆工商大学研二女生侯姝媛，凭着一股子闯劲儿，白手起家，成立了"517 骑行驿站"。如今，驿站广获骑行者好评，年营业额 60 多万元。

"有家的感觉""大学最后一次骑行""说走就走的旅行""告别雾霾，来海南骑行"

在驿站里，处处有骑友的留言，如今驿站已成为骑友的乐园。

建立驿站 2 年来，驿站的知名度不断提升。2013 年 6 月至今，已经有文昌、博鳌、兴隆 3 家旅店老板主动找上门来，成为 517 骑行驿站加盟店。

"去年我们有近 100 万元收入，纯收入 50 多万元，现在驿站已经布设环岛骑行线路的东线，预计 5 年后我们还会在环岛骑行的中线和西线开 5 至 10 家驿站，到时候骑友就会享受到我们一站式服务。"侯姝媛说。

说到新年打算，侯姝媛表示下一步将在环岛骑行的中线和西线开 5 至 10 家驿站，到时候骑友就能享受到更加便捷的服务，同时在跟旅行社洽谈合作，拟推出骑行旅游专线等。

如今，学校已开学，侯姝媛除了要经营好驿站，还要加强学习，她觉得在创业的同时不能将学业落下。

侯姝媛深信，"517 骑行驿站"一定能借助国际旅游岛建设步伐，生意将会越来越好。

（来源：https://www.360kuai.com/pc/）

Section III Case Analysis in Intercultural Communication

A British General Manager in Thailand

A British general manager upon arrival in Thailand refused to take his predecessor's car. The Thai finance manager asked the new GM what type of Mercedes he would like, then, the GM asked for a Suzuki or a Mini, anything that could be handled easily in the congested traffic in Bangkok.

Three weeks later the GM called the finance manager and asked about prospects for the delivery of his car. The Thai lost his reserve for a moment and exclaimed: "we can get you a new Mercedes by tomorrow, but Suzuki take much, much longer." The GM asked him to see what he could do to speed up the process. After four weeks the GM asked to see the purchase order for the car. The purchasing department replied that, because it would take so long to get a small car, they had decided to order a Mercedes.

The GM's patience had run out. At the first management meeting he brought the issue up and asked for an explanation. Somewhat shyly, the predominantly Thai management team explained that they could hardly come to work on bicycle.

Questions for discnssion

1. Why did the GM have difficulties in getting a Suzuki or Mini?
2. Why did the management team say they could hardly come to work on bicycle?

分析：泰国是等级观念很强的国家，泰国传统文化价值观的核心，如家长制、权威崇拜，等级观念等是人们日常行为所公认的准则，甚至是一种"生活方式"。人们认为社会等级制度对人有好处，所以不会向社会等级制度挑战。泰国的社会生活强调等级观念，依赖于等级关系。而在公司等社会机构中，强调正式的组织结构，各个等级保持一定的稳定性。

因此，在本案例中，最后泰国职员的解释是，如果总经理的用车降低水准，公司所有职员的用车要整体降级，最终有些职员必须要骑自行车上班，而这是他们不愿也无法做到的。在英国文化的价值观中，权力之间的距离很小。具体工作之外，人们之间是平等的，公司中的领导者用车是为了工作，为了提高业绩，因此英国经理看来，交通工具的选用是为了提高工作效率，每个人都有选择的自由，自己选用什么样的车与公司其他人无关。

Section IV *Practical Writing: Notice*

一、通知的形式

通知有多种分类。从形式上可分为书面通知（written notice）和口头通知（announcement）。书面通知用词正式，用大词较多，同时，用于书面化，可以使用一些长句；而口头通知以言简意赅为主要特点，用词表达较为口语化。

二、通知的结构

通知一般由标题、正文和结尾三部分组成。标题部分就是标题语；正文包括事情、通知对象、要求、时间、地点等；结尾部分主要包括落款和发通知的具体日期。英文通知的格式一般是将 NOTICE（每个字母都大写）写在通知正文上面一行的正中间。发通知的日期一般写在通知正文的左下角。

三、通知的书写

（1）发出通知的单位和对象在一般情况下用第三人称，如要求同学们按时到会，不说"we must to"或"you should"，而应写成：all the students are requested to be there on time. be expected/ supposed to do.

（2）书面通知常以布告形式张贴或写在布告牌、黑板上，把事情通知到有关人员等。为醒目起见，标题的每个字母可以用大写（如 NOTICE）。一开头需要交代说明何事（what）、何地（where）、何时（when）、何人（who）。

（3）在句式写法上必须注意以下几点：

①尽可能用精炼的文字表达明确的信息，多用简单句或短句、单句，以避免繁杂；

②通知往往着重对活动内容、对象进行说明，多用被动语态，如：The class meeting will be held.（班会将举行。）等；

③通知是要求下级成员该做什么或注意什么，多用祈使句；

④通知中所告的事情大部分是未进行的，故多用将来时态。

Sample

请按要求写一份英文通知：

外语系定于 2020 年 12 月 30 日下午 2:00 在校大礼堂举行每年一度的外语文艺节目汇报演出。内容包括：合唱、独唱、舞蹈、诗朗诵和小品等。热烈欢迎全体师生参与观看。

词数：60 词左右

NOTICE

The foreign language department takes pleasure in announcing its annual foreign language literary and artistic report performance, which is to be held in the university auditorium on December 30, 2020, at 2:00 p.m.. The program includes chorus, solo, dance, recitation and skit, all the teachers and students are warmly welcome.

Department of Foreign Languages
December 28, 2020

Practice

请你按要求书写一份英文通知：

你们学校在下周五（11月9日）19：00在校报告厅举行一场学术讲座，主要讨论如何有效学习英语。目前在美国西北大学任教的Johnson教授将应邀讲话。希望大家踊跃参加。

词数：60词左右

Section V *Grammar: Nominal Clause*（名词性从句）

在句子中起名词作用的句子叫名词性从句。名词性从句的功能相当于名词词组，它在复合句中能担任主语、宾语、表语、同位语，因此根据它在句中不同的语法功能，名词性从句又可分为主语从句、宾语从句、表语从句、同位语从句。

一、名词性从句的引导词

名词性从句的引导词可分为三类：从属连词、连接代词、连接副词。

1. 从属连词

引导名词性从句的从属连词有 as, as if, because, that, whether, if 等，that 与 whether/if 在从句中不充当任何成分，只起到引导从句的功能。that 没有实际意义，whether/if 意为"是否"。

例：That prices for vegetables will go up is certain. 蔬菜价格要上涨是确凿无疑的了。（that 引导主语从句，不作成分）

2. 连接代词

连接代词指既具有代词的特点，同时又能引导从句的词，主要有 what, whatever, who, whoever, whom, whose, which, whichever 等。这些词在从句中作特定的成分，有具体的含义，不能省略。

例：What we should do with the problem is undecided. 我们如何处理这个问题还未作出决定。（what 引导主语从句，表示疑问）

3. 连接副词

连接副词指既具有副词的特点，同时又能引导从句的词，主要有 when, where, how, why, whenever, wherever 等。这些词在从句中既作特定的成分，又有具体的含义，不能省略。

例：When I will meet you again is uncertain. 我何时才能再见到你还不确定。（when 引导主语从句，表示疑问）

二、主语从句

在句中起主语作用的从句称为主语从句。

1. that引导的主语从句

that 引导主语从句时，在从句中不作任何成分，也没有实际意义。一般情况下 that 不可省略。that 引导的主语从句置于句首。

例：That light travels in straight lines is known to all. 众所周知，光沿直线传播。

2. 形式主语it替代主语从句

that 从句作主语通常用 it 作形式主语，而将 that 从句置于句末。常见的 it 替代主语从句的句式主要有以下几种：

（1）it+ 系动词 + 形容词 +that 从句。

例：It is quite clear that the whole thing is a big lie. 整件事情就是一个大谎言，这是再清楚不过的事了。

（2）it+ 系动词 + 名词 + that 从句。

例：It is our purpose that the two sides will work towards peace.

我们的目的是双方能朝着和平的方向发展。

（3）it+ 系动词 + 动词的 -ed 形式 + that 从句。

例：It is reported that no passengers were injured in the earthquake. 据报道在地震中没有乘客受伤。

需要注意的是：

在 "it + be + suggested/advised/ordered/requested/required/insisted/demanded + that 从句" 结构中，that 从句应用 "should+ 动词原形"，其中 should 可省略。在 "It is necessary/important/surprising/strange/unthinkable/unbelievable/incredible+that 从句" 结构中，从句常

用 "should+ 动词原形" 形式，其中 should 可省略。

例：It is necessary that a college student (should) master one or two foreign languages. 大学生掌握一两门外语是必要的。

例：It is suggested that you (should) spend more time in studying English. 建议你花更多的时间学习英语。

3. wh-类连接词引导的主语从句

wh- 类连接词包括连接代词（who, whom, whose, what, whoever, whomever, whoever, whatever 等）和连接副词（when, where, how, why, whenever, wherever, however 等）。

例：Where we can find his key is still a problem. 我们在哪儿可以找到他的钥匙还是个难题。

三、表语从句

在句中作表语的从句称为表语从句。

1. that引导的表语从句

例：The point is that we lose the game. 关键是我们比赛失败了。

2. whether引导的表语从句

例：The question is whether we should help him. 问题在于我们是否应该帮助他。

3. wh-类连接词引导的表语从句

例：The problem is where we can find her. 问题是我们去哪里能找到她。

四、同位语从句

常见的可以跟同位语从句的名词主要是一些表示抽象意思的词。

advice 建议	belief 信念，相信	doubt 怀疑	explanation 解释
fact 事实	fear 害怕	feeling 感觉	hope 希望
idea 主意	news 消息	opinion 观点	order 命令
possibility 可能性	promise 答应，诺言	problem 问题	probability 可能性
question 问题	reply 答复	report 报道	suggestion 建议
thought 想法	truth 事实	wish 愿望	warning 警告

例：The news that he was going to retire was true. 他即将退休的新闻是真的。

五、宾语从句

在句子中起宾语作用的从句称为宾语从句。宾语从句可分为三类：v.+ 宾语从句、

Drop by drop the oceans are filled; stone by stone the walls are built. 滴水汇大海，垒石诛高墙。

prep.+ 宾语从句，adj.+ 宾语从句。

1. that引导的宾语从句（that没有具体含义，可以省略）

例：She said that she could finish her work before dinner.

她说她会在晚饭前完成工作。

2. if/whether引导的宾语从句

if/whether 引导宾语从句时，在从句中不作任何成分，但有具体含义，意为"是否"。不能省略。

例：We don't know if /whether he likes going swimming or not. 我们不知道他是否喜欢游泳。

3. wh-类连接词引导的宾语从句

例：Everybody wanted to know what the headmaster had said at the meeting. 每个人都想知道校长在会议上说了些什么。

* 重要提示

whether 与 if 均为"是否"的意思。但在下列情况下, whether 不能被 if 替代：

① 引导主语从句并置于句首时。

例：Whether he can come to the party on time depends on the traffic. 他是否能按时来参加晚会要看交通状况。

② 引导表语、同位语从句时。

例：The question is whether we can find her. 问题是我们能否找到她。

③ 引导介词后的宾语从句时。

例：I'm thinking about whether I can get in touch with Mary. 我正在考虑是否能联系到玛丽。

④ 后紧跟不定式或or not时。

例：He didn't know whether to laugh or to cry. 他不知道该哭还是该笑。

Exercise 1：Nominal clause（名词性从句）

一、单项选择

1. _____ they want to ask us to do is not clear.

A. What　　　　B. How　　　　C. Whether　　　　D. Why

2. The fact is _____ they have lost the chance to participate in the competition.

| A. that | B. what | C. how | D. which |

3. I don't care _____ the relationship works.

| A. what | B. that | C. why | D. whether |

4. It is unwise to give children _____ they want.

| A. whenever | B. whatever | C. whichever | D. however |

5. I am sure _____ they said is true.

| A. that | B. that what | C. of that | D. about that |

6. I have no idea _____ or not the children have finished their homework.

| A. if | B. that | C. whether | D. which |

7. _____ the employee didn't finish the task made his boss angry.

| A. That | B. What | C. Why | D. Whether |

8. _____ we'll go to the Great Wall this Sunday depends on the weather.

| A. If | B. Whether | C. That | D. Where |

9. That is _____ I come here so frequently.

| A. that | B. what | C. why | D. how |

10. What I'm worried about now _____ all the money we need.

| A. is | B. are | C. were | D. was |

11. Could you tell me _____?

A. who is that lady B. that lady is who
C. who that lady is D. whom is that lady

12. Do you know _____?

A. what is this box used for B. what this box is used for
C. which this box is used D. that this box is used for

13. My parents give me a lot of freedom. They let me do _____ I want.

| A. what | B. how | C. that | D. which |

14. _____ surprised me a lot was that he got the first prize.

| A. What | B. Whether | C. Why | D. Where |

15. Tom dropped out. I'll ask him why _____.

A. he has done so B. he did that
C. he did D. did he do that

16. I wonder how much _____.

A. the camera costs B. did the camera cost

C. the camera costed D. does the camera cost

17. _____ we will go to Shanghai will be discussed at tomorrow's meeting.

A. If B. What C. That D. Where

18. _____ you come with me or not depends on you.

A. Why B. If C. What D. Whether

19. The problem is _____ the task will be finished.

A. what B. when C. why D. who

20. That is _____ we once stayed.

A. what B. why C. that D. where

二、判断下列句子属于哪种名词性从句（主语从句、表语从句、宾语从句）。

1. The problem is that we are short of materials. (　　)

2. It is known to all that health is important. (　　)

3. What I like most in summer is watermelon. (　　)

4. I don't know what to do with my poor math. (　　)

5. Whether he understands me doesn't matter any longer. (　　)

6. What I did just now angered him a lot. (　　)

7. I am sure that he will overcome all the difficulties. (　　)

8. When he will arrive is still a mystery. (　　)

9. Could you tell me how to operate this machine? (　　)

10. Where the meeting will be held will be announced later. (　　)

11. The meaning of life depends on how you see it. (　　)

12. The fact is that we love peace. (　　)

13. It's necessary that you put on your coat when you are out in winter. (　　)

14. It is a pity that we do not know who we are anymore. (　　)

15. The doctor told me that I was well. (　　)

16. The truth is that he lied. (　　)

17. I'm glad that you are satisfied with our service. (　　)

18. That she will help you with your math is certain. (　　)

19. I'm afraid that the rain may be heavier. (　　)

20. Who will be the winner remains unknow. (　　)

三、翻译

1. 我不知道她爱吃什么。

2. 问题是我们怎样才能准时完成任务。

3. 他们来不来跟我没有关系。

4. 看上去天要下雪了。

5. 那就是为什么她那么喜欢粉色。

6. 我相信她不会骗我的。

7. 我想知道他跟你说了什么。

8. 他告诉我他下个月要去北京。

9. 我们想知道这个机器是如何运转的。

10. 让我感到震惊的是他们竟然没有告诉你这个消息。

11. 我们认为他不会这么做。

12. 我很高兴你相信我说的话。

13. 我担心我们可能会输掉比赛。

14. 谁对谁错还不清楚。

15. 我们无法确定他们是否会帮我们。

16. 生命的价值在于你做了什么。

17. 明天很可能会有大雨。

18. 据说他母亲离开北京了。

19. 我的建议是你好好休息下。

20. 请告诉我们你们想要什么。

扫一扫查看
练习参考答案

扫一扫查看
本章拓展资料

Unit 7

Volunteer

Learning Objectives

【About Knowledge】

1. To get to know about volunteering work.

2. To master useful words and expressions.

3. To talk about working as volunteers.

4. To know more about Attributive Clause.

【About Skills】

To know more about writing a Letter of Recommendation.

Section 1 Dialogues

Dialogue 1

Interviewing

A journalist from China Daily is interviewing a volunteer to talk about his experiences in volunteer work.

The journalist: Excuse me, I am a **reporter** of the **China Daily**. May I have a talk with you?

The volunteer: OK.

The journalist: I know you have been as a **volunteer** for ten years. Where do you usually do volunteer work?

The volunteer: I often volunteer at a hospital or work for a **local charity**, charity school for example.

The journalist: What do you do in charity school?

The volunteer: I often take part in the activities, like charity sale and **on-spot** donation.

The journalist: Yeah, these are **significative** things.

The volunteer: That is true. I like this kind of activity.

The journalist: Do you volunteer every week?

The volunteer: Yes, almost never stop.

Vocabulary and notes

1. reporter: n. a person who investigates and reports or edits news stories；记者

2. China Daily: 中国日报

3. volunteer: n. a person who performs voluntary work；志愿者；志愿兵

4. local: adj. relating to or applicable to or concerned with the administration of a city or town or district rather than a larger area；当地的，地方性的；局部的；局域的；本地通话的

5. charity: n. a foundation created to promote the public good (not for assistance to any particular individuals)；慈善；施舍；慈善团体；宽容；施舍物

6. on-spot: adj. 现场的；当场的

7. significative: adj. (usually followed by "of") pointing out or revealing clearly；有意义的；意味深长的；表示……的；为……提供推定证据的

Dialogue 2

Receiving a Delegation

*Sarah and her partners, the volunteers for the Shenzhen 26th Summer **Universiade**, are receiving Mr. Steven, the team leader of Australian Delegation.*

Sarah: Excuse me. Are you Mr. Steven, the team leader of Australian **Delegation**?

Mr. Steven: Yes, I am.

Sarah: Great! Let me introduce myself. I am a volunteer sent by the Executive Board for the Shenzhen 26th Summer Universiade. My name is Sarah .

Mr. Steven: Oh, wonderful! My name is John Steven. Nice to meet you.

Sarah: Glad to meet you too. Welcome to Shenzhen. We **are responsible for** guiding you all to the **designated** hotel, the **Pavilion Hotel**.

Mr. Steven: Thanks for coming to meet us.

Sarah: My pleasure. How was your trip?

Mr. Steven: It was pleasant **all the way**.

Sarah: That's great! So you have got all your team members here.

Mr. Steven: Yes. They are all here.

Sarah: Ok. **Everything's ready now**. Let's get on the bus. We will drive you to the Pavilion Hotel.

Mr. Steven: Well, where do we pick up the **luggage**?

Sarah: This way, please. Would you all please take your luggage and follow us?

Vocabulary and notes

1. Universiade: n. (the World University Games) The Universiade is an International multi-sport event, organized for university athletes by the International University Sports Federation (FISU). The name is a combination of the words "University" and "Olympiad"；世界大学生运动会

2. delegation: n. a group of representatives or delegates；代表团；授权；委托

3. be responsible for: 对……负责；是……的原因

4. designated: adj. marked, separated, or given a name for a particular purpose；指定的；特指的

5. Pavilion Hotel: 圣庭苑酒店（酒店名）

6. all the way: if you say that you go or travel all the way somewhere, you emphasize that it is a long way；一路上；自始至终；天长地久

7. everything's ready now: 一切都准备好了

8. luggage: n. a case used to carry belongings when traveling；行李；皮箱

📖 Dialogue 3

Lucy is talking with her friend, Ryan, about the charity and voluntary work.

Lucy: Did you read the recent story about Bill Gates and Warren Buffet, giving millions of dollars to the **charity** foundations they set up?

Ryan: I did read the story about Bill Gates and his wife, and how they are going to help the people of Africa, but, who is Warren Buffet?

Lucy: He's an American **billionaire** who made his money from investing.

Ryan: Well, it's good thing that they're using their money to help other people. After all, what can you really do with billions of dollars except to **make more money**?

Lucy: What do you think **motivates** people to be charitable?

Ryan: I **suppose**, that depends on the **individual**. Often, it's just the desire to help others. Sometimes it's an act of gratitude and, sometimes, it's just for the pleasure of giving.

Lucy: I saw that story about Liang Wenchong, who gave his 150,000 Yuan winner's prize, to help develop young golfers in China.

Ryan: That was a really **generous** gesture. There wouldn't be too many people who would do that sort of thing.

Lucy: I don't know. Think about all the people who volunteer to help others. They may not have much money to give but they can still help a lot of people.

Ryan: It's often said that it's better to give than to receive. Do you think that's true?

Lucy: That begs the question（这就是问题所在）. How do you get in the first place before you can give?

Ryan: Well, that's a thing. I hadn't thought of that.

Lucy: There is another saying I have heard. To quote, "If you can't look after yourself, what right do you have to look after anyone else?"

Ryan: I guess that's right. There's no point in the blind leading the blind.（盲人引导盲人是没有意义的）

Lucy: **Apart from** that, a lot of people have their pride and they resent being offered charity.

Ryan: That may be alright up to a point, but, if it's only yourself you have to worry about and you still have enough belief in your ability to **survive** then, go for it.

Lucy: If others depend on you then, sometimes, you have to face reality and don't let your pride get in the way of **accepting** a helping hand when it is offered.

Vocabulary and notes

1. charity: n. an organization that collects money and other voluntary contributions of help for people in need；慈善；施舍；仁爱；赈济

2. billionaire: n. somebody who has money and property worth more than a billion dollars or other currency; somebody who is extremely wealthy；亿万富翁；巨富

3. make money: 赚钱；发财

4. motivate: v. to make somebody feel enthusiastic, interested, and committed to something；激励；激发；成为……的动机；是……的原因

5. suppose: v. to consider or imagine something to be a possibility；假设；假定；设想；料想

6. individual: n. belonging to, relating to, or intended for one person only；个人；与众不同的人；有个性的人；某种类型的人

7. generous: adj. willing to give money, help, or time freely；慷慨的；大方的；慷慨给予的；丰富的

8. apart from: prep. except for someone or something；除了……外（都）；要不是；除了……外（还）；此外

9. survive: v. to remain alive or in existence or able to live or function, especially succeed in staying alive when faced with a life-threatening danger；生存；存活；幸存；继续存在

10. accept: v. to take something that is offered, e.g. a gift or payment；承认；接纳；同意；认可

Dialogue 4

Mike is a member of the World Peace Corps Volunteer Organization. He was sent to work as a high school teacher in Togo. A journalist is interviewing him, listening to him about that experience.

The journalist: Now, Mike, you were in the **Peace** Corps?
Mike: Peace Corps, yeah.

The journalist: Can you explain what the Peace Corps is and what you did?

Mike: Well, it's an organization, U.S. **Government** organization that sends young people, for the most part, college graduates, to different countries to work as volunteers in either **construction** or education. I was in education. I was a high school teacher.

The journalist: Where did you go? Which country?

Mike: I was in **Togo**.

The journalist: Togo?

Mike: It's a little country between Ghana and Dahomey, West **Africa**.

The journalist: West Africa, yeah.

Mike: And I was a high school teacher. I was an education major at the University of Michigan, and **trained** as a high school teacher there, but I had to get a **completely** different training, skills, to work in West African high schools. I must mention that the classes were huge, like a hundred students in a class, and we didn't have **textbooks**. We just had a blackboard in the front of the class and students only had notebooks, so you had to manage the class so that the students always had something to **write down**, or practice from their notebooks, and you know I had four or five classes like that every day, and it was a very **grueling** job, but very, very exciting work, I mean, I loved it. I just loved it. It was the best thing a college grad could do in my opinion.

The journalist: Have you ever gone back?

Mike: You know, I was just thinking about that the other day. I would love to. If I have the opportunity I will, or I have to make the opportunity to go back. It's a very **volatile** country, though, you know. But I don't think I would want to go there as a tourist, but I'd love to go back if I have an invitation to do something again.

The journalist: Alright, thanks Mike.

Mike: Sure.

Vocabulary and notes

1. peace: n. freedom from war, or the time when a war or conflict ends；和平；平静；宁静；和睦

2. government: n. a group of people who have the power to make and enforce laws for a country or area；政府；治理；政体；内阁

3. construction: n. the way in which something has been built, especially with regard to the

type and quality of the structure, materials, and workmanship；施工；建筑；建立；建造

4. Togo: n. country in West Africa, bordered by Burkina Faso, Benin, the Gulf of Guinea, and Ghana；多哥；（国）多哥；多哥共和国；位于西非

5. Africa: n. the second largest continent, lying south of Europe, with the Atlantic Ocean to the west and the Indian Ocean to the east；非洲

6. train: v. to learn the skills necessary to do a job, or teach somebody such skills, especially through practical experience；训练；培训；教育；接受训练

7. completely: adv. if something is done completely, every part of it is done；（用以强调）完全地

8. textbook: a book that treats a subject comprehensively and is used by students as a basis for study；教科书

9. write down: to record something in writing, usually so that the information will not lost or forget；记下来

10. grueling: adj. extremely arduous or exhausting；使极度疲劳的

11. volatile: adj. apt to become suddenly violent or dangerous；易变的；无定性的；无常性的；可能急剧波动的

Activity

Make up a dialogue based on the following situation.

Suppose you have been a volunteer for the China Import & Export Commodities Fair in 2019, a journalist from China Daily wants to have an interview with you, talking about your volunteering work during the fair.

Section II Extensive Reading

  Passage 1

Volunteering

Volunteering means spending some of your free time helping others. You may volunteer to help other people, and you can also volunteer to **protect** animals, the environment, or any other things that you **care** about.

Volunteering helps others, and it can also help you. If you're **worried about** something that's happened, doing something else can be a great way to deal with（处理）your **feelings**.

Volunteering can let you see your own life in new ways. Sometimes it's easy to worry about things like **grades** or get angry because you don't have the most **expensive** shoes or the newest computer game. Volunteering let you spend some time on others for a while.

Lots of people find that they really enjoy volunteering. Volunteer **experiences** often put you in a different environment. Doing volunteer work means one very important thing: You can make a difference in the world.

Volunteering is a great way to have fun with your family, and here are some ideas on what you can do together.

- Clean up a park, or a road along a river.
- Plant trees or flowers in your **community**（社区）.
- Serve food at a homeless **shelter**（收容所）.
- Give meals to people who are **elderly** or ill at home.
- Clean up a school or other public buildings.

Some schools now require（要求）kids to spend some of their time on service to others. Volunteering gives kids a sense of **responsibility**, because people are depending on them for something important. Volunteering also can help kids learn important things about themselves. A volunteer job can even help some kids decide what they want to do when they grow up. So what are you waiting for? Make a plan to start volunteering today!

Vocabulary and notes

1. protect: v. to prevent somebody or something from being harmed or damaged；保护；防护；（制定法律）保护

2. care: v. to be interested in or concerned about something；关心；关怀；在意；关注

3. be worried about: 担心；为……担心

4. feeling: n. an emotional state, for example anger or happiness；感觉；感情；知觉；看法

5. grade: n. a class or year in a school, especially in the U.S. and Canadian school systems；品级；水平；评分等级；阶段

6. expensive: adj. costing a large amount of money；昂贵的；花钱多的；价格高的

Empty vessels make the greatest sound. 空桶响声大。

7. experience: n. active involvement in an activity or exposure to events or people over a period of time that leads to an increase in knowledge or skill；体验；经历；实践；阅历

8. community: n. a group of people who live in the same area, or the area in which they live；社区；社团；公众；社会团体

9. shelter: n. a place where people are protected from bad weather or from danger；避难所；庇护所；躲避；住所

10. elderly: adj. past middle age and approaching the later stages of life；年纪较大的

11. responsibility: n. the state or job of being in charge of someone or something and of making sure that what they do or what happens to them is right or satisfactory；责任；职责；负责；义务

12. Volunteering helps others, and it can also help you. If you're worried about something that's happened, doing something else can be a great way to deal with（处理）your feelings. 志愿服务可以帮助别人，也可以帮助你自己。如果你担心已经发生的事情，那么找点事做可以很好地缓解你的情绪。

13. Lots of people find that they really enjoy volunteering. Volunteer experiences often put you in a different environment. Doing volunteer work means one very important thing: You can make a difference in the world. 很多人发现他们真的很喜欢做志愿者。志愿者的经历常常让你置身于不同的环境中。做志愿者工作意味着一件非常重要的事情：你能改变世界。

14. Volunteering also can help kids learn important things about themselves. A volunteer job can even help some kids decide what they want to do when they grow up. So what are you waiting for? Make a plan to start volunteering today! 志愿服务也可以帮助孩子们了解什么对自己来说是重要的。一份志愿者工作甚至可以帮助一些孩子决定他们长大后想做什么。那么你还等什么呢？今天就开始做志愿者吧！

📖 译文

志愿者工作

志愿工作意味着把你的一些空闲时间花在帮助别人上。你可以自愿帮助别人，也可以自愿保护动物、环境或其他你关心的事情。

志愿服务可以帮助别人，也可以帮助你自己。如果你担心已经发生的事情，那么找点事做可以很好地缓解你的情绪。

志愿服务可以让你以新的方式看待自己的生活。有时候，你很容易担心成绩之类的事情，或者因为你没有最贵的鞋子或最新的电脑游戏而生气。志愿服务让你可以在别人身上花上一段时间。

很多人发现他们真的很喜欢做志愿者。志愿者的经历常常让你置身于不同的环境中。做志愿者工作意味着一件非常重要的事情：你能改变世界。志愿服务是一个可以与你的家人一起获得快乐的很好的方式，这里有一些志愿服务活动，你们可以一起参与。

- 清理公园或沿河道路。
- 在社区种植树木或花卉。
- 在无家可归者收容所提供食物。
- 为年老或因生病而待在家中的人提供膳食。
- 清理学校或其他公共建筑。

一些学校现在要求孩子们把一些时间花在为他人服务上。志愿工作给孩子们带来责任感，因为人们在一些重要的事情上依赖于他们。志愿服务也可以帮助孩子们了解什么对自己来说是重要的。一份志愿者工作甚至可以帮助一些孩子决定他们长大后想做什么。那么你还在等什么呢？今天就开始做志愿者吧！

Passage 2

Volunteering and its Surprising Benefits

Volunteering can help you make friends, learn new skills, **advance** your career, and even feel happier and healthier. Learn how to find the right fit.

Why volunteer?

With busy lives, it can be hard to find time to volunteer. However, the **benefits** of volunteering can be **enormous**. Volunteering offers vital help to people in need, **worthwhile** causes, and the community, but the benefits can be even greater for you, the volunteer. The right match can help you to find friends, **connect** with the community, learn new skills, and even advance your career.

Giving to others can also help protect your **mental** and physical health. It can reduce stress, **combat** depression, keep you mentally stimulated, and provide a sense of purpose. While it's true that the more you volunteer, the more benefits you'll experience, volunteering doesn't have to involve a long-term commitment or take a huge amount of time out of your busy day. Giving in even simple ways can help those in need and improve your health and happiness.

Volunteering connects you to others

One of the more well-known benefits of volunteering is the impact on the community. Volunteering allows you to connect to your community and make it a better place. Even helping out with the smallest tasks can make a real difference to the lives of people, animals, and organizations in need. And volunteering is a two-way street: it can benefit you and your family as much as the cause you choose to help. Dedicating your time as a volunteer helps you make new friends, expand your social network, and boost your social skills.

Make new friends and contacts

One of the best ways to make new friends and strengthen existing relationships is to commit to a shared activity together. Volunteering is a great way to meet new people, especially if you are new to an area. It strengthens your ties to the community and broadens your support network, exposing you to people with common interests, neighborhood resources, and fun and fulfilling activities.

Increase your social and relationship skills

While some people are naturally outgoing, others are shy and have a hard time meeting new people. Volunteering gives you the opportunity to practice and develop your social skills, since you are meeting regularly with a group of people with common interests. Once you have momentum, it's easier to branch out and make more friends and contacts.

（来源：https://www.helpguide.org/）

Vocabulary and notes

1. advance: v. to move, or move somebody or something, forward in position；提前；进步；促进；预付

2. benefit: n. something that has a good effect or promotes well-being；益处；优势；成效；福利费（政府对失业者、病人等提供的补助金）

3. enormous: adj. unusually large or great in size, amount, or degree；巨大的；大量的；庞大的

4. worthwhile: adj. rewarding or beneficial enough to justify the time taken or the effort made；重要的；令人愉快的；有趣的；值得花时间（或花钱、努力等）

5. connect: v. to make a psychological or emotional association between people, things, or events；连接；接通；沟通；联结

6. mental: adj. relating to, found in, or occurring in the mind；思想的；精神的；思考的；智力的

7. combat: v. to attempt to destroy or control something harmful；战斗；防止；减轻；与……搏斗

8. expand: v. to become or make something become larger in size, scope, or extent, or greater in number or amount；扩大；扩展；详述；细谈

9. boost: v. to improve, strengthen, or encourage somebody or something；使增长；使兴旺；偷窃

10. contact: n. a state or relationship in which communication happens or is possible；接触；联络；交往；接触器

11. existing: adj. used for describing something that exists now, especially when it might be changed or replaced；现存的；现行的

12. broaden: v. to enlarge the range or magnitude of something, or become wider in range or magnitude；变宽；变阔；（使）扩大影响；增长（经验、知识等）

13. expose: v. to put somebody or something in a vulnerable or potentially dangerous situation；暴露；揭露；曝光；揭穿

14. With busy lives, it can be hard to find time to volunteer. However, the benefits of volunteering can be enormous. 由于生活繁忙，很难有时间做志愿者。然而，志愿服务的好处是巨大的。

15. While it's true that the more you volunteer, the more benefits you'll experience, volunteering doesn't have to involve a long-term commitment or take a huge amount of time out of your busy day. 诚然，你做志愿者的次数越多，你得到的好处就越多，但志愿工作不必涉及长期的承诺，也不必从繁忙的一天中抽出大量的时间。

16. And volunteering is a two-way street: it can benefit you and your family as much as the cause you choose to help. Dedicating your time as a volunteer helps you make new friends, expand your social network, and boost your social skills. 志愿服务是双向的：它不仅可以让你选择自愿服务的事业受益，也可以让你和你的家人受益。把你的时间奉献给志愿活动可以帮助你结交新朋友，扩大你的人际网络，提高你的社交能力。

📖 译文

志愿服务及其惊人的好处

志愿服务可以帮助你交朋友,学习新技能,促进你的事业,甚至让你感到更快乐、更健康。学习如何找到合适的志愿者活动。

为什么做志愿者?

由于生活繁忙,很难有时间做志愿者。然而,志愿服务的好处是巨大的。志愿服务为有需要的人、有价值的事业和社区提供了至关重要的帮助,但对你这个志愿者来说,好处可能更大。适配的志愿者活动可以帮助你找到朋友,与社区建立联系,学习新技能,甚至可以促进你的事业。

给予行为也能促进你身心健康发展。它可以减轻压力,对抗抑郁,让你精神振奋,不再漫无目的。诚然,你做志愿者的次数越多,你得到的好处就越多,但志愿工作不必涉及长期的承诺,也不必从繁忙的一天中抽出大量的时间。即使是简单的方式,给予也能帮助那些需要帮助的人,并改善你的健康和提升你的幸福感。

志愿服务把你和其他人联系起来

志愿服务一个众所周知的好处是对社区的影响。志愿服务可以让你与你的社区建立联系,使之成为一个更好的地方。即使是帮助完成最小的任务,也能对需要帮助的人、动物和组织的生活产生实质性的影响。志愿服务是双向的:它不仅可以让你选择自愿服务的事业受益,也可以让你和你的家人受益。把你的时间奉献给志愿活动可以帮助你结交新朋友,扩大你的人际网络,提高你的社交能力。

结交新朋友

结交新朋友和加强现有关系的最好方法之一就是共同参与一项活动。当志愿者是结识新朋友的好方法,尤其是当你初到一个地方。它加强了你与社区的联系,拓宽了你的支持网络,让你接触到有共同兴趣的人,获得邻里资源,参与有趣而有成就感的活动。

提高你的社交和人际关系技能

虽然有些人天生外向,但有些人很害羞,很难结识新朋友。志愿工作让你有机会练习和发展你的社交技能,因为你经常与一群志同道合的人见面,一旦你有了动力,就更容易扩大活动范围,结交更多的朋友和人脉。

Section III Case Analysis in Intercultural Communication

Different Philosophies

Dr Richard Lowry, a prominent American engineer, was commissioned by a company in Indonesia to direct (with a local construction supervisor) a bridge-building project in the interior of the country. Before departing, Dr. Lowry studied the Indonesian language and customs of the people he would be working with. He also studied Islamic religion since he knew that the Indonesian supervisor was a devout Muslim. Although he adjusted well to the local community, there were aspects of his work to which he had trouble adapting. Material never seemed to be available when it was supposed to be. Workers seldom showed up on time for work, and when they did, they were slow to get started. The relationship with the Indonesian supervisor was far from perfect. They could not seem to agree on a schedule for the arrival of goods. In fact, it did not seem that his partner even cared about completing the project at the desired time. Midway through his three-month assignment Dr. Lowry became so frustrated and moody.He became less productive, kept to himself and frequently thought about returning home.

（来源：汪福祥，马登阁. 文化撞击——案例评估 [M]. 北京：石油工业出版社，1999.）

Questions for discussion

What is the primary cause for the problem above? Does it result from their different philosophies on management or different world views?

分析：来自不同国家或不同宗教的人们拥有不同的世界观。他们对待工作和问题有着不同的看法和解决方法，这种差异使劳瑞博士感到困惑。尽管他来印尼之前已经学习了一些当地语言和风俗习惯，但他对印尼的文化结构知之甚少。如果他能够多待上一段时间，深入了解印尼人民的行为所依据的不同哲学，多了解穆斯林文化，便可更轻松地应对。

Even the walls have ears. 隔墙有耳。

Section IV Practical Writing: Letter of Recommendation

推荐信是一个人为推荐另一个人去获得某个职位、参与某项工作或求学等而写的信件，常用于留学申请和求职等。

基本格式和要求：

（1）推荐者姓名、职位、单位名称、地址等。

（2）简单介绍推荐人自己的背景、自己与被推荐人的关系、推荐他/她的目的。

（3）陈述被推荐人的工作经历或个人特点，如在工作、学习、为人、性格等方面的优点。重点突出他/她的技术、完成的任务、对公司或社会的贡献等。结尾部分向收件人表示感谢和期待。

信件寄送方式可以是书信，也可以是电子邮件。可依据对方具体要求而定。

正文内容可包含：

（1）为便于对方查阅、归档，正文部分应尽快提及被推荐者的全名，其所用字母、大小写、连写和分写等拼写法，应与被推荐人的申请信或简历上的拼写法完全相同。

（2）开宗明义，表明态度，说明自己乐意推荐某人，自己同被推荐人之间的关系。

（3）接下来可介绍与推荐人何时认识、熟悉程度、有何联系等内容。

（4）正文中的重点是对被推荐人的人品、能力、性格特点作介绍。尽可能做到言简意赅，点面结合。

（5）正文的最后部分，一般以提出建议作为结束，即推荐人建议校方或用人单位对被推荐人的申请惠予考虑，录取或聘用被推荐人。有时，也可就对方接受自己的推荐表示谢意结束全文。

（6）签名之后应注明推荐人的职衔或职称。如果使用的是普通信笺，而不是带有信头的公文信笺，不便于对方联系，最好在职衔或称呼之下再注上推荐人的通讯地址（包括单位名称、地址、电话、邮政编码等）。

Sample

Dear Mr. Brown,

  It is my pleasure to recommend Li Ming, my good friend, for his application to work in your company. Li Ming graduated from Beijing Industry University. His major is Computer Software. During the four years' study he has done a good job. Every year he got the first grade scholarship. And he also has got the title of the Excellent Graduate. He is an enthusiastic and progressive young man with high potentiality. He is not only quick at learning but also good at solving difficult problems with logical mind. I am sure that it will benefit your company if he can work for your company. I strongly recommend him to your company.

Yours Sincerely,
Wang Lin

Practice

假如你是王林，李明是你的好友，他对布朗先生的公司感兴趣，打算到该公司谋职（apply for a position）。请根据下面李明的简历表，用英语为他写一封推荐信。

姓名：李明　性别：男　　　国籍：中国

出生地：重庆　婚否：已婚　　出生日期：1980.8.21

职业：律师　学历：大学毕业

外语水平：擅长英语，懂一些日语、德语

其他：有三年工作经历，办事认真，待人诚恳，与人和睦相处

注意：

1. 词数 100 左右。

2. 可以适当增加细节，以使行文连贯。

Every cloud has a silver lining. 山穷水尽疑无路，柳暗花明又一村。

Practice

Dear Mr. Brown,

Section V *Grammar: Attributive Clause*（定语从句）

担任定语功能的句子称为定语从句，定语从句较为复杂，学习定语从句的过程中要做好以下几点：

（1）正确判断先行词。
（2）准确使用关系词。
（3）准确区分定语从句与名词性从句、状语从句。
（4）掌握定语从句与定语、状语之间的转化。

一、关系词的用法

定语从句所修饰的词叫先行词；连接先行词与从句的词叫关系词。定语从句一般由关系代词或关系副词来引导，关系词不仅在先行词与定语从句之间起连接作用，而且在从句中充当一定的成分。

引导定语从句的关系代词有 that, who, whom, whose, which, as；关系副词有 when, where, why。各关系词及其具体用法见下表：

关系词	词形	所修饰的先行词	在从句所作的成分
关系代词	who	人	主语、宾语
	whom	人	宾语
	which	物	主语、宾语
	that	人或物	主语、宾语、表语
	as	人、物或事	主语、宾语
	whose	人或物	定语
关系副词	when	时间名词	时间状语
	where	地点名词	地点状语
	why	原因名词	原因状语

1. 关系代词的用法

关系代词起到指代先行词的作用，在定语从句中作主语、宾语、表语等。作宾语时，口语中常省略；如果关系代词作介词的宾语且介词提到关系代词的前面时，关系代词不能省略。

（1）who (m) 的用法。

二者都用于指人。who 在定语从句中作主语、宾语，whom 在定语从句中作宾语。

例：He is the man who (m) I am looking for. 他就是那个我正在寻找的人。（作宾语）

需要注意的是在从句中作介词的宾语且直接跟在介词后时，只能用 whom，不能用 who。

例：Yesterday I came across the man about whom you talked last time. 昨天我偶然遇到了你上次提到过的那个人。

（2）whose 的用法。

whose 一般指人，但有时也指物，在定语从句中作定语。

例：Do you know the girl whose English is excellent? 你认识那个英语非常优秀的姑娘吗？（作定语）

（3）which 的用法。

which 一般指物，在定语从句中作主语、宾语，也可作定语。

例：The train which has just left is for Shanghai. 刚开走的火车是开往上海的。

例：This is the book that/which you are looking for. 这正是你在找的那本书。（作宾语）

（4）that 的用法。

that 可指人或物，指人时可与 who，whom 互换，指物时可与 which 互换。在从句中可作主语、宾语、表语。作宾语时可以省略，作介词的宾语时，介词不可提到 that 之前，若介词提前则须用 which 或 whom 等其他词替代。

例：Jone is no longer the person that/which I met four years ago. 琼不再是四年前我见到的琼了。

例：The book which/that you are looking for is about to sell out. 你正在找的那本书会卖完了。

（5）as 的用法。

as 引导定语从句主要用于两种情况：一种是限制性定语从句，先行词有 so，such 或 the same 等修饰；一种是先行词是整个主句的非限制性定语从句。

①引导先行词前有 as, so, such, the same 修饰的限制性定语从句：

当先行词前有 as, so, such, the same 等修饰时，在从句中作主语或宾语的关系代词用 as。

例：I want the same books as my brother bought the day before yesterday. 我想要一本同我哥哥前天带来的一样的书。

②引导先行词是整个主句的非限制性定语从句：

例：As we had expected, the plan worked out very well. 正如我们预料的，这个计划运行得非常好。

2. 关系副词的用法

（1）where 的用法。

where 指地点，在从句中作地点状语。它的先行词通常为 place, spot, street, house, room, city, town, country 等表示地点的名词。where 引导的定语从句还可以放在 from 后。

例：This is the mountain village I stayed last year. 这就是我去年待过的山村。

例：Please put the books in a place you can find them easily. 请把书放在容易找到的地方。

（2）why 的用法。

why 指原因，它的先行词只有 reason，在定语从句中作原因状语。

例：This is the reason why he refused our help? 这就是他拒绝我们帮助他的理由。

例：I come to explain the reason why I was late from the meeting. 我来是为了解释我开会迟到的原因。

（3）when 的用法。

when 指时间，在从句中作时间状语。它的先行词通常为 time, day, morning, night, week, year 等表示时间的名词。

例：I still remember the day when I first came here by plane. 我仍然记得第一次坐飞机来这里的那一天。

例：Do you know the date when the PRC was founded? 你知道中国人民共和国成立的日子吗？

二、限制性定语从句和非限制性定语从句

限制性定语从句用来修饰和限定先行词，与先行词间的关系非常密切，不用逗号和主句隔开。它所修饰的先行词代表一个（些）或一类特定的人或物，说明先行词的性质、身份、特征等状况，如果去掉，则意思含糊不清。而非限制性定语从句，就是对先行词没有特别限定的从句，常由 who, whom, which, whose, as, when, where 等关系词引导。用逗号和主句隔开，that 不能用来引导非限制性定语从句。

例：My car, which I bought last year, has got beautifulcolour. 我的汽车是去年买的，颜色很漂亮。（非限制性定语从句，可有可无）

例：I have a brother who is a doctor. 我有一个当医生的哥哥。（可能有几个哥哥，其中一个是医生）（限制性定语从句）

三、宜用that不宜用which的情况

（1）当先行词是 all, little, few, much, something, anything, everything, nothing, none, some 等不定代词时：

例：I did everything that I could help him. 我做了一切能做的事来帮助他。

（2）先行词被 all, every, no, some, any, little, much, the only, the very, the right, the last, few, just 等词修饰时：

例：This is the very picture that I want. 这正是我想要的图片。

（3）先行词是序数词或形容词最高级或被序数词、形容词最高级修饰时：

例：This is the most interesting book that I have ever read. 这是我读过的最有趣的书。

（4）当先行词既有人又有物时：

例：The audience spoke highly of the play and the players that they saw at the theatre. 观众们高度赞扬了他们在剧院看到的这些演员以及他们的表演。

四、宜用which不宜用that的情况

（1）关系代词前有介词时：

例：The school in which I used to study has become a stadium. 我以前上学的学校现在变成了体育馆。

（2）在非限制性定语从句中（见非限制性定语从句讲解）。

（3）先行词本身就是 that 时：

例：I don't like that which he did. 我不喜欢他做的那件事。

Exercise：Attributive Clause（定语从句）

一、单项选择

1. The building _____ interested me most was the Forbidden City.

　　A. in which　　　B. where　　　　C. what　　　　　D. which

2. This is the library _____ last week.

　　A. which we visited　　　　　　B. to that we visited

　　C. where we visited to　　　　　D. where we visited

3. May 10th, this is the day _____ I'll never forget for the rest of my life.

　　A. which　　　　B. on which　　　C. in which　　　D. when

4. Could you lend me the album _____ last week?

　　A. that you talked　　　　　　　B. which you talked

　　C. about that you talked　　　　 D. about which you talked

5. The designer _____ my sister works is about 30 years old.

　　A. with whom　　　　　　　　B. on whom

　　C. with which　　　　　　　　 D. to whom

6. We are satisfied with _____ you have done.

　　A. all that　　　B. all what　　　C. that　　　　　D. which

7. She isn't such a lady _____ she used to be.

　　A. who　　　　B. whom　　　　C. that　　　　　D. as

8. They talked a lot about things and persons _____ they remembered in the university.

　　A. whom　　　B. that　　　　　C. which　　　　D. what

9. The gift is from my friend, _____ is studying in Shanghai.

A. whom　　　　B. that　　　　C. which　　　　D. who

10. He was not the man _____ he was before.

A. where　　　　B. who　　　　C. that　　　　D. what

11. Last week, we tasted the Beijing Roast Duck, _____ Beijing is famous in the world.

A. for which　　　B. for that　　　C. in which　　　D. what

12. The way _____ they look at this problem is not correct.

A. what　　　　B. whose　　　　C. which　　　　D. /

13. I'm certain that this is the reason _____ she didn't come to my birthday.

A. for which　　　B. with which　　　C. that　　　　D. in which

14. We are working hard, _____ will make us pass the English Test.

A. that　　　　B. for which　　　C. which　　　　D. who

15. Anyone _____ breaks the rules will without doubt be dismissed.

A. who　　　　B. that　　　　C. which　　　　D. whom

16. She is not one _____ gives up easily.

A. who　　　　B. that　　　　C. which　　　　D. whom

17. We ought to do all _____ is helpful to the people.

A. that　　　　B. who　　　　C. which　　　　D. /

18. There are two seats in the front row _____ is available.

A. that　　　　B. who　　　　C. which　　　　D. /

19. This is the latest film about _____ they are talking.

A. that　　　　B. who　　　　C. which　　　　D. /

20. He passed the exam, _____ means a lot to him.

A. /　　　　B. who　　　　C. which　　　　D. that

二、选择适当的关系词填空

1. I believe Jack will be the one _____ (who/that) will win the first prize.

2. The ones _____ (that/who) cheat in the exam will be punished.

3. Those _____ (who/that) don't like to walk around can stay here, waiting for us.

4. She has a daughter, _____ (who/whom) is a teacher.

5. This is the most brilliant palace _____ (which/that) I have ever visited.

6. I want to go back to the place _____ (where/which) I was born.

7. I can't figure out the reason _____ (why/that) she didn't come with us.

8. I don't like the way _____ (that / which) he talked to the stranger.

9. Are you familiar with the lady _____ (whom/which) I talked to just now?

10. This is one of the best films _____ (that/which) I have ever seen this month.

11. Is there anyone in our class _____ (whose/who) family is in Hangzhou?

12. Tom, with _____ (who/whom) I went to the theater enjoyed it very much.

13. I lost my purse, _____ (which/whose) color is pink.

14. This is the reason _____ (why/that) he didn't finish the task on time.

15. The man _____ (which/who) run into the store is Jack's brother.

16. You should think twice before believing whatever promise _____ (that/when) he makes.

17. All _____ (that/which) can be done has been done on time.

18. The most important thing _____ (which/that) we should keep in mind is that health matters.

19. _____ (As/ That) is known to everybody, the moon travels round the earth once every month.

20. On the door hung a bell, _____ (whose/which) color is golden yellow.

三、翻译

1. 我们昨天遇到的那个女孩是汤姆的妹妹。

2. 昨天你买的相机是今年最新款。

3. 我买了一本书，它的封面是蓝色的。

4. 《泰坦尼克号》是我看过的最好看的电影。

5. 这就是我选择英语专业的原因。

6. 我想回到我们第一次相遇的地方。

7. 我是那个会坚持到最后一刻的人。

8. 那些努力付出的人总会有所收获的。

9. 我有一个律师朋友。

10. 所有想说的话我一句都说不出来了。

11. 她是我想陪伴到老的人。

12. 你昨天说的话还算数么？

13. 你家墙上挂的画是我最喜欢的一幅作品。

14. 你喜欢昨天她提到的那本书么？
15. 我不知道为什么她突然改变主意。
16. 很多人不喜欢他对老板说话的方式。
17. 昨天跟我哥哥交谈的那位叫做汤姆的人是一名警察。
18. 所有看过这部电影的人都被感动得眼泪直流。
19. 成功属于那些永不言弃的人。
20. 我昨天买的票丢了。

扫一扫查看
练习参考答案

扫一扫查看
本章拓展资料

Every man has his faults. 人孰无过。

Module 3
The Culture of the Forests

Unit 8

Mountain Trip

扫一扫查看
本章教学PPT

Learning Objectives

【About Knowledge】

1. To get to know how to invite sb. to mountain climbing.

2. To master useful words and expressions.

3. To talk about mountain trips.

4. To know more about Adverbial Clause.

【About Skills】

To know more about the written request for a leave.

Section 1 *Dialogues*

Dialogue 1

Planning of a Mountain Trip

Lucy is talking with her friend, Ryan, about her plan to Tanzhe Temple.

Lucy: I want to spend two days in the **mountains** with friends. The city is too noisy. Do you know Tanzhe **Temple**?

Ryan: I have been there before. It is **in the middle of** the mountains. It is quiet and tranquil and you have to be a **vegetarian** in your stay there.

Lucy: Do you want to climb the mountain with us?

Ryan: Is there enough **lodging**?

Lucy: No problem. The temple is quite large.

Ryan: There are many **ancient** pine trees there. It is especially quiet at night. It is wonderful to listen to the monks chanting while listening to the soothing sound of the winds in the pine trees.

Lucy: I'm getting a little excited now. What clothes should I wear?

Ryan: Take some thick clothes with you. It is rather cold there at night. If you wear the T-shirt you're wearing, you will become a "**Popsicle**".

Lucy: Anything else I should take?

Ryan: If you like taking pictures, you may take a camera with you.

Lucy: **Needless to say**.

Vocabulary and notes

1. mountain: n. a natural structure like a very big hill that is much higher than the usual level of land around it；山；高山；山脉；山岭

2. temple: n. a building used for worship in some religions, typically religions other than Christianity；庙宇；圣殿

3. in the middle of: 正在……当中；在……的中途；在……的中央

4. vegetarian: n. somebody who eats vegetables, fruits, grains, seeds, and usually eggs and dairy products, but not meat or fish；素食者；吃素的人

5. lodge: v. to make a formal complaint, accusation, or appeal by handing the documents to the appropriate authority；（向公共机构或当局）正式提出（声明等）；借宿；租住

6. ancient: adj. very old；古代的；古老的；很老的

7. popsicle: n. [Brands and Products, Food] a piece of sweet flavored ice on a stick, mainly used in American English；（商，食）冰棍；冰棒

8. needless to say: it is used for saying that something is already known or understood；不用说

Dialogue 2

A Trip in Guilin

Han lei is a tour guide. He is telling his tourists about their tour in Guilin.

Every man is the son of his own works. 种瓜得瓜，种豆得豆。

Han Lei: Hi! Good morning, everybody! My name is Han Lei. I will be your **tour** guide for your trip in Guilin.

The tourist: It seems there are so many beautiful **sceneries** in Guilin. What are we going to see first?

Han Lei: Today we are going to visit Elephant Trunk Hill.

The tourist: Elephant Trunk Hill? Sounds interesting.

Han Lei: Right, literally speaking, the hill looks like a giant elephant drinking water with its **trunk** in the Li River.

The tourist: Are we going to take a boat ride in the Li River today?

Han Lei: No. We will try it tomorrow because the boat ride is a one-day trip.

The tourist: Oh, I can't wait to take the boat ride. There is a saying goes like this "The mountains and waters of Guilin are the finest under **heaven**."

Han Lei: You are **absolutely** right. **Seeing is believing**. You will see it yourself tomorrow. OK, let's go to the Elephant Trunk Hill first.

The tourist: Ok. Let's go.

Han Lei: Here we are. Look! That is Elephant Trunk Hill. You can see that between the trunk and the legs there is a moon-**shaped** cave.

The tourist: I see **halfway** up the hill there is a cave which goes through the hill. Does that serve as the eyes of the elephant?

Han Lei: Yes. That is the eye of the elephant. On top of the hill stands a **pagoda** named Puxian Pagoda, built in the Ming Dynasty (1368-1644).

The tourist: Could you do me a favor?

Han Lei: sure.

The tourist: Could you take a picture for me?

Han Lei: Ok. S-m-i-l-e!

The tourist: Thank you so much.

Han Lei: You are welcome. Let's move to our next stop Reed Flute **Cave**.

The tourist: Hooray!

Vocabulary and notes

1. tour: n. travel through；旅游；旅行；参观；游览

2. scenery: n. landscape or natural surroundings, especially when regarded as picturesque；风景；景色；风光

3. trunk: n. the main part of a tree that the branches grow out of and also the long nose of elephant；树干；躯干；象鼻

4. heaven: n. a place or condition of supreme happiness and peace where good people are believed to go after death, and, especially in Christianity, where god and the angels are believed to dwell；天堂；天国；天空；极乐之地

5. absolutely: adv. used to give strong emphasis to what is being said；完全地；绝对不；完全没有；极其

6. seeing is believing: 眼见为实；百闻不如一见；眼见为凭

7. shaped: adj. formed by changing something's original or natural shape；具有（或呈）……形状的

8. halfway: adj. equal in distance from two places or from the two ends of something 中间的

9. pagoda: n. a Buddhist temple building, especially one in the form of a tower with several stories, each with an upward curving roof that tapers slightly toward the top；（南亚或东亚的）佛塔

10. cave: n. a large, naturally hollowed-out place in the ground, or in rock above ground, that can be reached from the surface or from water；洞穴；山洞

Dialogue 3

Mountain Climbing

Susan is talking about her mountaineering experience with her friend, David.

Susan: Are you **interested in** mountaineering?

David: Yes, to some extent, I should say I like mountain climbing because I'm not so **professional**. How about you?

Susan: I'm **the same with you**, an **amateur** mountain climber. I went climbing in the Rocky Mountains with my friends last summer vacation. We spent two days in the mountains.

David: How did you spend the night there?

Susan: We pitched a **tent** in the night, waiting for the **sunrise**. Wow! It was really beautiful.

David: I had a **similar** experience, but that was on the top of Taishan Mountain in my country.

Every pleasure has a pain. 乐中必有苦。

Susan: Taishan Mountain? It's very famous in China, isn't it?

David: Yes. It is one of the Five Mountains.

Susan: I want to climb Taishan Mountain this summer vacation. Would you be my **guide**?

David: I'd love to.

Vocabulary and notes

1. be interested in: v. 对……感兴趣

2. professional: adj. conforming to the standards of skill, competence, or character normally expected of a properly qualified and experienced person in a work environment；职业的；专业的；有职业的；娴熟的

3. the same with you: 和你一样

4. amateur: adj. done in an unskillful or unprofessional way；业余爱好的；业余的

5. tent: n. a collapsible movable shelter consisting of a tough fabric or plastic cover held up by poles and kept in place by ropes and pegs；帐篷；帐棚

6. sunrise: n. the rising of the sun above the eastern horizon each morning；日出；朝霞

7. similar: adj. sharing some qualities, but not identical；类似的；相像的；相仿的

8. guide: n. somebody who leads and assists others in a place or toward a destination；向导；导游；手册

Dialogue 4

Go Hiking in Mountains

Todd is chatting with his friend, Leo, about Leo's hobby.

Todd: So, Leo, what do you like to do in your free time?

Leo: Um, free time. Well, I'd just love to have some free time, **occasionally** I have some free time and well, I love to **go hiking**. Ah, I live in Japan in Kyuushuu（九州）and there are some beautiful mountains quite nearby, so sometimes I go hiking in the mountains.

Todd: Well, actually, I love hiking and I am new to Kyuushuu. I just moved here, so can you tell me where I should go hiking. What are the best **spots**?

Leo: Well, there's a range of mountains in Kuju. One of the mountains is called Nakadake, which means central peak, I believe, and that is actually the highest peak, the highest mountain on **mainland** Kyuushuu. There is one higher mountain on an **island** near Kagoshima but on mainland Kyuushuu that's the highest peak and it's quite a challenge and there are some beautiful views from that mountain.

Todd: Wow! Can I make it in one day?

Leo: Oh, sure. It takes about three hours to go up the mountain while the **descent** only takes about two hours.

Todd: Oh, that's great. We live in Beppu（九州别府）and it is **on the coast**. Unfortunately, I don't have a car, so how can I get to the mountain?

Leo: Um, I'm absolutely not sure. I've only ever been there by car myself. Um, I don't believe there's a train that stops by the mountain, but you can certainly get closer than you are now by train, and then you can **perhaps** take a bus or even a taxi from a town closer by. I'm sorry. I'm afraid I could offer no help.

Todd: Oh, that's OK. Well, you know, I've never done it before, but I hear that it's safe to **hitchhike** in Japan. Is that true?

Leo: Oh, absolutely. Yep. The crime rate in Japan is low. You'd have to be **incredibly** unlucky to have any problems hitchhiking.

Todd: And will people stop and pick me up?

Leo: Ah, I don't know.

Todd: Maybe I'll have to give it a try. OK, thanks a lot.

Leo: You're welcome.

Vocabulary and notes

1. occasionally: adv. from time to time, but not regularly or frequently；偶尔；有时候；偶然

2. go hiking: 去远足；去徒步旅行；去徒步远足

3. spot: n. a specific place or area 地点；场所；处所

4. mainland: n. the principal landmass of a continent or country as distinct from its islands, and sometimes also excluding its peninsulas；大陆；（不包括附近岛屿的）国土的主体

5. island: n. an area of land, smaller than a continent, that is completely surrounded by water；岛

6. descent: n. an act of going from the top to the bottom or from a higher position to a lower position；下降；血统；祖先；斜坡

7. on the coast: 沿海

8. perhaps: adv. used to show approximation；也许；可能；大概；如果

9. hitchhike: v. to travel by asking other people to take you in their car, by standing on the side of a road and holding out your thumb or a sign；搭便车（旅行）

10. incredibly: adv. extremely；非常；极其；难以置信地；不可思议地

Activity

Make up a dialogue based on the following situation.

Make a dialogue with your partner about your mountain trip during the vocation.

Section II Extensive Reading

Passage 1

The Mount Wuyi

Mount Wuyi is located in the north of Fujian Province and the city Wuyishan is named for this mountain. Mount Wuyi is one of the most **outstanding subtropical** forests in the world. It is the largest, most representative example of a largely intact forest encompassing the diversity of the Chinese Subtropical Forest and the South Chinese Rainforest. It acts as a **refuge** for a large number of ancient, relict plant species, many of which are endemic to China and contains large numbers of reptile, amphibian and insect species. In 1988 it **was listed as** one of the world's biosphere protection areas. With its great scenery and wealth of cultural **relics**, in December 1999, Mount Wuyi was put on the list of World Cultural and Natural Heritage by the UN World Heritage Committee, thus becoming the fourth in China after Mount. Taishan, Mount. Huangshan, and Mount. Emei.

One of the main natural landscapes in this area, Nine-twist Stream（九曲溪）is named for its shape that a stream runs as a **curve** which has nine bends. It looks like a dragon around the mountain. It takes about 2 hours to drift down the stream **by means of** a very old type of bamboo raft（竹筏）. During the two hours, you can enjoy the beautiful **landscapes**, which contains many famous scenic spots of Mount Wuyi, including, king of peaks, the sight, waterfall cave, etc. So this experience is **unique** and memorable. No visitor could miss the chance. The peak (king of peaks) is shaped like an ancient Chinese **majestic** official's hat, so people call it Great King Peak. It is majestically located at the mouth of Jiuqu Creek（九曲）, Southeast of Mount Wuyi. It stands on the 530 meters' peak to welcome the departing tourists.

Located south of the second twist and facing a big deep pool, the Jade Maiden Peak looks like a girl standing gracefully. The rock in Jade Maiden Peak appears skin-smooth while the **dewy**-green grass and tree sat the top suggest a girl's hair. As we look at the peak's reflection in the water, we can imagine a graceful, deep-in-thought, ancient girl, wishing for a bright future. This peak symbolizes the beauty of Wuyi scenery.

Now, let's go to the last part: Cultural heritage. First a mysterious funeral ceremony: Hanging Coffins. The hanging coffin was a custom of the local people. They think the pillar is more closed to the heaven. When people were died, they would be hung on the man-made or natural cave. The higher he was hung, the more respectable he was. But until today we don't know how the original people put these heavy coffins up to the steep cliff. It's a mystery.

Vocabulary and notes

1. outstanding: adj. clearly of very high quality or clearly superior to others in the same group or category；杰出的；尚待解决的；突出的

2. subtropical: adj. relating to or found in areas between tropical and temperate regions, and experiencing tropical conditions at some times of the year or nearly tropical conditions all year round；亚热带的；副热带的

3. refuge: n. a sheltered or protected state safe from something threatening, harmful, or unpleasant；避难所；庇护；慰藉；庇护者

4. be listed as: 被列为

5. relic: n. something that has survived from a long time ago, often a part of something old that has remained when the rest of it has decayed or been destroyed；遗迹；遗物；遗风；遗俗

6. curve: n. a line that bends smoothly and regularly from being straight or flat, like part of a circle or sphere；曲线；弯曲；曲面；弧线

7. by means of: 用；依靠；借助于

8. landscape: n. an expanse of scenery of a particular type, especially as much as can be

seen by the eyes；景色；乡村风景画

9. unique: adj. being the only one of a kind；唯一的；独一无二的；独特的；罕见的

10. majestic: adj. big, beautiful, or impressive in a calm and serious way；宏伟（的）；威严（的）；从容大方；不可一世

11. dewy: adj. wet with drops dew 露水打湿的；带露水的

12. It is the largest, most representative example of a largely intact forest encompassing the diversity of the Chinese Subtropical Forest and the South Chinese Rainforest. 这是最大最具代表性的一个完整无损的森林，涵盖了中国亚热带森林和华南雨林的多样性。

13. In 1988 it was listed as one of the world's biosphere protection areas. With its great scenery and wealth of cultural relics, in December 1999, Mount Wuyi was put on the list of World Cultural and Natural Heritage by the UN World Heritage Committee, thus becoming the fourth in China after Mount. Taishan, Mount. Huangshan, and Mount. Emei. 1988 年它被列为世界生物圈保护区之一。武夷山风景秀丽，文物丰富，1999 年 12 月被联合国世界遗产委员会列入世界文化和自然遗产名录，成为继泰山、黄山、峨眉山之后的中国第四大自然遗产。

14. During the two hours, you can enjoy the beautiful landscapes, which contains many famous scenic spots of Mount Wuyi, including, king of peaks, the sight, waterfall cave, etc. So this experience is unique and memorable. 在这两个小时内，您可以欣赏到美丽的风景，这里有许多著名的武夷山景点，包括大王峰、景观、瀑布洞等，因此这一体验是独特难忘的。

15. The hanging coffin was a custom of the local people. They think the pillar is more closed to the heaven. When people were died, they would be hung on the man-made or natural cave. 悬棺是当地人的风俗习惯。他们认为山峰更接近天堂。人死后，会被悬在人工或天然的洞穴上。

武夷山

武夷山位于福建省北部，武夷山市因这座山而得名。武夷山是世界上最著名的亚热带森林之一。这是最大最具代表性的一个完整无损的森林，涵盖了中国亚热带森林和华南雨林的多样性。它为大量古老的、残余的植物物种提供了庇护所。这些植物物种中许多是中国特有

的。此外，这里还栖息着大量的爬行动物、两栖动物和昆虫物种。1988年它被列为世界生物圈保护区之一。武夷山风景秀丽，文物丰富，1999年12月被联合国世界遗产委员会列入世界文化和自然遗产名录，成为继泰山、黄山、峨眉山之后的中国第四大自然遗产。

九曲溪是该地区主要的自然景观之一，因其形状如一条有九个弯道的曲线而得名。它看起来像一条龙，缠绕着山。乘坐古老的竹筏顺流而下大约需要两个小时。在这两个小时内，您可以欣赏到美丽的风景，这里有许多著名的武夷山景点，包括山峰之王、景观、瀑布洞等，因此这一体验是独特难忘的，任何游客都不应该错过。这座山峰（山峰之王）的形状像中国古代的一顶威严的官帽，人们称之为"大王峰"，气势宏伟，位于武夷山东南九曲溪河口，矗立在530米高的山峰上欢迎起程的游客。

玉女峰位于第二个拐弯处的南面，面对一个巨大的深潭，宛如一个亭亭玉立的少女。玉女峰的岩石光滑，顶部的露水青草和树木像女孩的头发。当我们看到山峰在水中的倒影，我们可以想象是一个优雅、沉思、古老的女孩希望有一个光明的未来。这座山峰代表了武夷山的美丽。

现在，让我们来到最后一站：文化遗产。首先是一个神秘的葬礼：悬棺。悬棺是当地人的风俗习惯。他们认为山峰更接近天堂。人死后，会被悬在人工或天然的洞穴上。他被悬放得越高，就越受人尊敬。但直到今天，我们还不知道人们当初是如何把这些沉重的棺材放到陡峭的悬崖上的。这是个谜。

📖 Passage 2

About Mount Tai

Mount Tai in Shandong province was listed as "**World Natural and Cultural Heritage**" by **UNESCO**（世界文化和自然遗产）in Dec 1987.

Mount Tai, a typical representative of the Chinese famous traditional mountains, is a mountain with a long history and a special historic status. In 1982, Mount Tai was up into the list of State Key Scenic Spots（国家重点旅游景点）and was formally listed as the World Natural and Cultural Heritage in 1987. It becomes a precious heritage of human being. Mount Tai is located in the east of North China Plain and the middle of Shandong province **erecting** from the Shandong hills. It is prominent around other hills. The **prominent** peak, Yuhuang Peak, is 1545 meters high and is located at 117.6 degree East longitude（东经）, 36.16 degree north latitude（北纬）. The south of Mount Tai is higher than the north. Its southern foot of mountain begins from Tai'an city and its northern foot of mountain stops in Jinan City, the distance between which is 60kms. The transportation there is convenient with the Jinghu railway passing by in the west. In its north is Jinan city, which has another name of "Spring City". The distance between Mount Tai and Qufu is 70 kilometers. Many roads and railways such as Taifei, Taixin and Taining meet in Tai'an city, which is just located in the south of Mount Tai.

Mount Tai is in a superior **geographic** location with abundant water and thermal resources, and it belongs to monsoon climate of medium latitudes（温带季风气候）. As regard to its historic position, in the ancient times, Mount Tai is a developed region——in the lower reaches（下游）of the Yellow River. As regard to its cultural position, it is the center of Dongyi Culture. At the southern foot of Mount Tai, there is Dawenkou Culture, and there is Longshan Culture at its northern foot, it is the center of Qi and Lu. And its transportation is more superior. Mount Tai is in a key position where the railway from central plains to Shandong **peninsula** meets the railway connecting the south and north of the east coast. There are no hills between Mount Tai and the capitals in the ancient times as well as the developed **regions**. This superior condition helps Mount Tai gain the first position among the Five Sacred Mountains in China.

As a mountainous scenic spot, Mount Tai has high values in terms of aesthetics（美学）and science, especially the aesthetic value, which is the foundation for Mount Tai to become a famous mountain in the history and the World Natural and Cultural Heritage today. For thousands of years, during the process of studying on Mount Tai in terms of adoration, taste（审美）, religion and science, the people have created extremely abundant and valued Taishan scenic culture. Moreover, in the Taishan scenic culture, the natural scene **plays the key role** with the literacy scene assisting. The nature and culture penetrate into each other. Here we can see the ideas of philosophy, aesthetics and science about the **harmonious** development of Heaven, Earth and Mankind. Thereby, either from the point of time or space, Mount Tai contains extremely abundant contents with high aesthetic, scientific and historic value. We can say that Mount Tai is the **symbol** of Chinese spiritual culture and the unique heritage of the world.

Vocabulary and notes

1. World Cultural and Natural Heritage: 世界文化与自然遗产

2. heritage: n. the status, conditions, or character acquired by being born into a particular family or social class；遗产（指国家或社会长期形成的历史、传统和特色）

3. UNESCO: abbr. [International Organizations] (=United Nations Educational, Scientific and Cultural Organization) a United Nations agency that promotes international collaboration on

culture, education, and science；（组）联合国教科文组织

4. erect: v. to build a structure from basic parts and materials；建立；建造；竖立

5. prominent: adj. distinguished, eminent, or well-known；重要的；著名的；杰出的；显眼的

6. geographic: adj. relating to geography or to the geography of a specific region；地理学的

7. peninsula: n. a narrow piece of land that juts out from the mainland into an area of water；半岛

8. region: n. a large land area that has geographic, political, or cultural characteristics that distinguish it from others, whether existing within one country or extending over several；区域；行政区

9. play the key role: 发挥关键作用

10. harmonious: adj. characterized by friendly agreement or accord；友好和睦的；和谐的；协调的

11. symbol: n. something that stands for or represents something else, especially an object representing an abstraction；符号；象征

12. It becomes a precious heritage of human being. Mount Tai is located in the east of North China Plain and the middle of Shandong province erecting from the Shandong hills. 它成为人类宝贵的遗产。泰山位于华北平原的东部，山东省中部，从山东丘陵耸立而起。

13. In its north is Jinan city, which has another name of "Spring City". The distance between Mount Tai and Qufu is 70kms. Many roads and railways such as Taifei, Taixin and Taining meet in Tai'an city, which is just located in the south of Mount Tai.北面是济南市，又称"泉城"。泰山和曲阜之间的距离是 70 公里。泰肥、泰辛、泰宁等多条公路、铁路在泰安市交汇（泰安市位于泰山南麓）。

14. As regard to its historic position, in the ancient times, Mount Tai is a developed region——in the lower reaches（下游）of the Yellow River. 就其历史地位而言，泰山在古代是一个发达地区——位于黄河下游。

15. As a mountainous scenic spot, Mount Tai has high values in terms of aesthetics（美学）and science, especially the aesthetic value, which is the foundation for Mount Tai to become a famous mountain in the history and the World Natural and Cultural Heritage today. 泰山风景区山峦绵亘，在美学和科学上都有很高的价值，尤其是审美价值，是泰山成为历史名山和世界自然文化遗产的基础。

📖 译文

泰山

山东泰山于1987年12月被联合国教科文组织列为《世界自然与文化遗产名录》。泰山是中国传统名山的典型代表,具有悠久的历史和特殊的历史地位。1982年,泰山被列入国家重点风景名胜区名录,1987年正式列入《世界自然与文化遗产名录》。它成为人类宝贵的遗产。泰山位于华北平原的东部,山东省中部,从山东丘陵耸立而起。与周围的山峦相比,泰山显得尤为突出。最著名的山峰玉皇峰海拔1545米,位于东经117.6度,北纬36.16度。泰山南高北低。南麓起于泰安市,北麓止于济南市,相距60公里。西面有京沪铁路经过,交通十分便利。北面是济南市,又称"泉城"。泰山和曲阜之间的距离是70公里。泰肥、泰辛、泰宁等多条公路、铁路在泰安市交汇(泰安市位于泰山南麓)。

泰山地理位置优越,水热资源丰富,属温带季风气候。就其历史地位而言,泰山在古代是一个发达地区——位于黄河下游。就其文化地位而言,它是东夷文化的中心。泰山南麓有大汶口文化,北麓有龙山文化,是齐鲁的中心。而且它的交通更优越。泰山是中原通往山东半岛的铁路与连接东海岸南北的铁路交汇处。泰山与古都和发达地区之间没有山丘。这种优越的条件使泰山在中国五大神山中独占鳌头。

泰山风景区山峦绵亘,在美学和科学上都有很高的价值,尤其是审美价值,是泰山成为历史名山和世界自然文化遗产的基础。千百年来,人们在对泰山的崇拜、审美、宗教、科学等方面的研究过程中,创造了极为丰富和珍贵的泰山风景文化。此外,在泰山风景文化中,自然景观起着关键作用,文化景观起辅助作用。自然与文化相互渗透。在这里,我们可以看到关于天、地、人和谐发展的哲学、美学和科学思想。因此,无论从时间还是空间上看,泰山蕴藏着极其丰富的内容,具有极高的美学价值、科学价值和历史价值。可以说,泰山是中国精神文化的象征,是世界的独特遗产。

Section III *Case Analysis in Intercultural Communication*

Respect for Seniority

After a week's training, I came to the place where I would live for a year-Busan, South Korea. According to the original arrangement, I should be picked up by a teacher of the school from the Department of Education. Due to the change of school system in South Korea, she was not qualified for business trip. I was also a new teacher who had just arrived at the school. Therefore, Mr. Zheng, the former Chinese teacher, would meet me temporarily. Mr. Zheng's Chinese was very good. He was friendly and approachable. He told me a lot about the school and the students along the way, which made me prepared for the new life here .

When I arrived , I didn't even have time to put the suitcase I took to South Korea within a five-minute drive from the school. I was told that the first thing I had to do was to go to the school to see the principal and supervisor. I asked Mr. Zheng if I could put my luggage in my room first and tidy up so that I could take out the gifts for the principal and the supervisor, and it would be more convenient for us to move. But Mr. Zheng's reply to me was, "First, according to the Korean tradition, we should report to our leaders at the first time. It is also polite to see the principal and the supervisor at the first time. Second, although we arrived on the day of rest, It is just the school supervisor's work that you should visit the school. As for the principal who does not go to work today, he may not go to see you for the time being. To see the supervisor of the school can be regarded as knowing the rule. Third, the school's off-duty time is 4:40 p.m. If we go back to the room to put your luggage, you will arrive just a few minutes before the school supervisor leaves work. This is also impolite." I was convinced by the reasons listed by Mr. Zheng.

We really should do as the Romans do in Rome and keep the local customs. After all, it is not polite in China to visit your boss a few minutes after work.

Question for discussion

Why did Mr. Zheng ask me to see the principal and the supervisor at the first time?

分析：韩国社会普遍推崇地位高、权力大的人，人们以入学年份、入职时间区分前辈和晚辈，以身份地位确定尊卑贵，形成了一套清晰的等级规定。等级尊卑的价值观可以说是韩国社会的主流价值观。在这种价值观的主导下，韩国人有着一套复杂而严苛的尊卑礼仪。以职场为例，职场中，职员入职时首先要拜见大领导，然后再依次见过直属领导和前辈同事们，晚辈对长辈、下级对上级要毕恭毕敬，说话要用敬语；职员遇见领导要鞠躬致意，走路要避让，吃饭时要主动为领导和前辈倒酒，倒酒或递东西时要用右手或双手，上级责骂下级，前辈责骂晚辈，下级和晚辈都要服从和接受，这些都是韩国人约定俗成的礼仪规约。案例中郑老师接到远道而来的王老师，不先送王老师到住的地方安顿下来，而是载着王老师和大包小包的行李先到学校向校监报到的做法也就合乎常理了——韩国严格的尊卑礼节使然。

Extremes meet. 否极泰来。

Section IV *Practical Writing: Written Request for a Leave*

请假条（written request for leave）是英语学习者必须掌握的常用应用文之一，它包括请病假（note for sick leave）和请事假（leave of absence）。请假条是用于向老师或上级领导等因身体状况不好或因某事请求准假的场合。

英文请假条写作需注意三点：

（1）英文中请假条的写法和汉语请假条相同，它一般由四部分组成，即时间、称呼、正文和签名。

（2）一般而言，可认定请假条是一种简单的书信文体。请假条一般写在纸上，不用信封。其书写格式与书信有很多相似之处，是书信的大大简化。

（3）请假条的特点是要求开门见山、内容简短、用词通俗易懂。

假如你是王立。昨天你和同学们去农场帮助农民们摘苹果，不幸（unluckily）从梯子上摔下来伤了腿，但伤得不重。医生让你在家里好好休息。因此，你向高老师请假两天（ask for a leave for two days）。

Sample

Sept. 28th

Dear Miss Gao,

    I'm sorry I can't go to school today. I helped the farmers pick apples with my classmates on the farm yesterday. Unluckily, I fell off the ladder and hurt my leg, but I wasn't badly hurt. the doctor asked me to stay in bed and have a good rest, so I ask for leave for two days. I hope you can grant my leave.

                                                       Your student

                                                       Wang Li

分析：这是一份采用书信格式写的请假条。日期是 September 28，日期写在正文的右上角。由于请假条的内容大多是当天、近几日因病或因事请假，所以不必写上年份；称呼是 Dear Miss Gao，称呼写在左上角。请假条因是向上级请示，一般以 Dear...，或 My dear... 开头。有时可在 dear 之后，用上 Mr 或 Miss 等的称呼加上姓氏。

不过，有一点仍要提醒大家，各种称呼后面一般都用逗号。正文谈了一件事：I fell off the ladder and hurt my leg, but I wasn't badly hurt. I can't come to school. I ask for leave for two days. 简洁明了，用词口语化。写请假条只要把请假的理由和请假时间说清楚即可。

有的请假条为了说明其请假事由是真实的，在正文之后另起一行，写上 I enclose a doctor's certificate.（我附上了医生证明。）；签名为 Wang Li。签名（署名）写在右下角，签名（署名）上面一行可以写上 Yours, Your student 等字样，有时由于写条的人和收条的人彼此一般很熟悉，所以在称呼和签名上比较随便和简单。特别是在签名部分，有时可简单到只写个姓或只写个名就可以了。

Useful expressions

（1）I am sorry to ask for a **sick/business/absence/ maternity/ long/ medical** leave of XX days.

（2）I am **very/really/extremely/terribly/awfully** sorry to tell you that I cannot attend/come to your XX class today.

（3）I am very/awfully sorry that…

（4）I have to go to see the doctor.

（5）I want to **ask for** four days' leave from Tuesday to

（6）I hope you can **grant my leave**.

（7）Please excuse me for my absence.

（8）I hope you can **excuse my absence**.

Enclose the doctor's certificate or other proofs

（1）Enclosed please find a certificate form.

（2）I submit here a medical certificate from the hospital.

（3）I enclose a doctor's certificate of advice.

> **Practice**
>
> Wang Hai is a student in Fujian Forestry Technical & Vocational College. His supervisor invited him to attend an academic meeting in Beijing on Oct. 24-25. Now write to his English teacher, Ms. Chen, asking for 3 days leave from the class from Oct. 23-25.
>
> Dear Ms. Chen,

Section V *Grammar: Adverbial Clause*（状语从句）

在复合句中修饰主句中的动词、形容词、副词等的从句叫状语从句，一般可分为时间状语从句、地点状语从句、原因状语从句、目的状语从句、结果状语从句、条件状语从句、让步状语从句、比较状语从句、方式状语从句等。

一、时间状语从句

在句子中起时间状语作用的句子称为时间状语从句。时间状语从句可以放在句首、句中和句尾。常用引导词有 when, while, as, before, after, until/till, as soon as, since, each time, next time, the moment, immediately, instantly 等。

（1）when 引导的时间状语从句和 while 引导的时间状语从句的区别：

when 意为"当……时"，引导时间状语从句，表示主句的动作和从句的动作同时或先后发生，从句中的动词可以用延续性动词，也可以用短暂性动词；while 引导时间状语从句时，意为"与……同时，在……期间"，从句常用延续性动词或表示状态的动词。

例：I feel very happy when you come to see me. 你们来看我时，我感到很高兴。

例：He was doing homework when I went in. 我进去的时候，他正在做作业。

例：I was watching TV while my husband was reading last night. 昨晚我在看电视的时候我的先生在看书。

（2）as 引导的时间状语从句，as 引导时间状语从句时，可以表达"正当；一边……一边……；随着"等意思。

例：They walked into the classroom as the bell stopped. 铃声一停，他们就走进了教室。

（3）before 引导的时间状语从句，before 意为"在……之前，多长时间后才……，用不了多长时间就……"，引导时间 状语从句时，表示主句的动作发生在从句的动作之前。

例：I cleaned my room before I left home yesterday. 昨天离开家之前，我打扫了自己的房间。

（4）after 引导的时间状语从句，after 意为"在……之后"，引导时间状语从句时，表示主句的动作发生在从句的动作之后。

例：After you read the books, you mustn't throw them about. 在读过书之后，不准到处乱扔。

（5）since 引导的时间状语从句，since 引导状语从句时意为"自从……"，主句常用现在完成时，从句常用一般过去时。

例：I have not seen him since we met last year. 自从去年我们见面后，我就再也没见到他。

常用句型"It is/has been+ 时间段 +since 从句"可译为"自从……有多长时间了"。

例：It is/ has been five years since she left hometown. 自从她离开家乡已有五年的时间了。

（6）until/till 引导的时间状语从句，主句是肯定句时，谓语须用延续性动词，表示动作一直持续到 until/till 表示的时间为止，until/till 意为"直到……为止"；主句是否定句时，谓语须用非延续性动词，表示主句的动作直到 until/till 表示的时间才发生，not...until/till 意为"直到……才。

例：I'll stay here until you come back. 我会待在这里，直到你回来。（stay 表示的动作可以持续）

例：We won't begin our competition until/till he comes. 直到他来了我们才能开始讨论。（start 表示的动作不能持续）

（7）as soon as 引导的时间状语从句，as soon as 意为"一就"，表示从句的动作一发生，主句的动作马上就发生。

例：Please tell him about it as soon as he comes back. 他一回来告诉他这件事。

二、地点状语从句

在句中作地点状语的从句称为地点状语从句，常由 where, wherever 等引导。地点状语从句可置于句首、句中或句尾。

例：Finally I found all the missing books where I had left them. 最后我在丢东西的地方找到了所有丢失的书籍。

三、原因状语从句

在句中作原因状语的从句称为原因状语从句。原因状语从句可置于句首，也可置于句尾。常用引导词主要有 because, as, since 等；短语引导词主要有 now that, for the reason that, in that, seeing that, considering (that) 等。

because, since, as 引导的原因状语从句的区别：because 表因果关系的语气最强，常用来回答 why 的提问，所引出的原因往往是听话的人不知道的或最感兴趣的；since 引导的原因状语从句表示人们已知的事实，不需要强调的原因，故常译成"既然……"，通常放在句首，since 引导的从句是次要的，重点强调主句的内容；as 引导的原因状语从句和 since 用法差不多，所引出的理由在说话人看来已经很明显，不需要强调。

例：They like me because I am helpful and kind. 因为我乐于助人且很友好，所以他们都很喜欢我。

例：Sine you are free now, why not take a walk with me? 既然你现在有空，为什么不和我出去走走呢？

例：As you are in bad mood, you should relax yourself. 既然你情绪不好，你就应该放松一下自己。

四、目的状语从句

在句中作目的状语的从句称为目的状语从句。常用引导词有 so, so that, in order that, for fear that, in case (that), for the purpose that, lest 等。目的状语从句可置于句首、句中或句尾，且从句中常有情态动词 could, might, should 等。

例：The teacher raised his voice in order that the students in the back could hear more clearly. 老师提高了声音，以便坐在后面的学生能听得更清楚。

例：Take an umbrella with you in case it rains. 你最好把雨伞戴上，以防下雨。

五、结果状语从句

在句子中作结果状语的从句称为结果状语从句。结果状语从句一般置于句尾。常用引导词或短语有 that, so, so that, so... that... , such... that... 等。

例：She worried about her son so that she couldn't sleep. 她担心她的儿子结果失眠了。

六、条件状语从句

在句子中作条件状语的从句称为条件状语从句。可置于句首、句尾或者主语和谓语之间。常用引导词有 if, unless, as/so long as, once, in case, on condition that, supposing (that), providing (that), provided (that) 等。在条件状语从句中，通常用一般现在时表示一般将来时，一般过去时表示过去将来时，现在完成时表示将来完成时。

例：If you tell him, he will tell his mother. 如果你告诉他，他就会告诉他妈妈。

七、让步状语从句

常用引导词有 although, though, as, even if/ though, while, whether, whatever, no matter what/how/why 等。

例：She is generous though she is poor. 她很穷，但很慷慨。

例：We'll take a trip even if/even though the weather is bad. 即使天气不好，我们也要去旅行。

还有方式状语从句，比较状语从句等，就不一一列举了。

Exercise 1：Adverbial Clause（状语从句）

一、单项选择

1. _____ he's young, he knows a lot about philosophy（人生哲学）.
   A. So　　　　　B. Since　　　　　C. For　　　　　D. Though

2. We will stay at home if my grandparents _____ to visit us this Sunday.
   A. is coming　　B. come　　　　　C. will come　　D. comes

3. I was late for meeting yesterday _____ my car broke down on the way.
   A. because　　　B. that　　　　　C. until　　　　D. when

4. You will be late for the meeting _____ you leave right away.

   A. if   B. until   C. unless   D. or

5. Remember to write to me as soon as you _____ to Shanghai.

   A. get   B. will get   C. getting   D. got

6. The football match will be canceled（取消）if it _____ tomorrow.

   A. will rain   B. rains   C. rained   D. is raining

7. It is 10 years _____ the bridge was built.

   A. after   B. before   C. when   D. since

8. _____ the boss entered the meeting room, all the employees closed their mouths.

   A. The moment   B. Before   C. Till   D. For

9. Not until I began to volunteer _____ how meaningful it is to give.

   A. didn't I realize   B. did I realize   C. I didn't realize   D. I realized

10. It was _____ it snowed heavily that they got lost in the woods.

    A. because   B. as   C. for   D. since

11. It is eight months _____ I left the university.

    A. since   B. after   C. when   D. as

12. _____ I saw the car, I was into it.

    A. The first time   B. For the first time   C. Until   D. At first

13. My boss was _____ busy in his working _____ he often missed his meals.

    A. enough, as   B. so, that   C. such, as   D. very, that

14. She must be ill, _____ she looks so pale.

    A. as   B. because   C. since   D. for

15. I'll stay here and wait for you _____ you come back.

    A. until   B. since   C. and   D. while

16. You will have a cold _____ put on more clothes in such a cold winter.

    A. if you   B. if you will not   C. unless you   D. until you

17. You must finish your homework _____ you go out to play with your classmates.

    A. when   B. after   C. before   D. while

18. The boss raised his voice _____ all the workers could hear him.

    A. because   B. so that   C. for   D. in order

19. She put on her coat _____ she felt cold.

A. if		B. as		C. because		D. since

20. _____ I felt very uncomfortable, I tried to sit the exam.

A. As		B. Because		C. Although		D. As if

二、根据中文意思完成下列英语句子

1. 不管他说什么，我都不会改变主意的。

   I will not change my mind, _____ he says to me.

2. 布莱克太太对邻居非常好，以至于大家把她非常喜欢她。

   Mrs Black is _____ kind to her neighbors _____ they like her very much.

3. 只要我们永不放弃，我们就能取得成功。

   We will succeed _____ _____ _____ we never give up.

4. 你一到家就给我打个电话。

   Please call me _____ _____ _____ you get home.

5. 这个七岁的女孩在她三岁的时候就开始练习弹钢琴了。

   The seven-year-old girl has learned to play the piano _____ she was three years old.

6. 虽然他很忙，他还每天坚持运动。

   _____ _____ _____ _____, he keeps on doing exercise every day.

7. 我长大后想当一名老师。

   I want to be a teacher _____ _____ _____ _____.

8. 无论刮风下雨，我们的老板总是第一个到公司。

   _____ _____ windy or rainy, our boss is always the first to get to the company.

9. 如果人人都献出一点爱，世界将会变得更美好。

   _____ _____ _____ _____ _____ _____ _____, the world will become much better.

10. 昨天的篮球赛延期了，因为下雨了。

    The basketball match was put off yesterday, _____ _____ _____.

11. 有志者事竟成。

    _____ there is a will, there is a way.

12. 如果你不想说的话，可以保持沉默。

    _____ _____ _____ _____ _____ _____ _____ _____ _____, you can choose to keep silent.

13. 为了开会，我从北京飞到上海。

I flew from Beijing to Shanghai _____ _____ _____ attend a meeting.

14. 毕业后我成立一名工程师。

_____ _____ I became an engineer.

15. 离开教室的时候请记得关灯。

Please remember to turn off the lights _____ _____ _____ _____ _____.

16. 三思而后行。

Think _____ you leap.

17. 即使你很年轻，你也需要锻炼身体。

_____ _____ you are young, you still need to workout（锻炼）.

18. 直到今天我才完成我的家庭作业。

I finished my homework _____ today.

19. 主席一走进会议室，所有人都起立。

_____ _____ the president entered the conference room（会议室）, everyone stood up.

20. 小孩子应该从小养成好习惯。

Children should develop good habits _____ _____ _____ _____.

三、翻译

1. 长大后我想当一名律师。

2. 无论天气如何，我们都准时到学校。

3. 虽然他很聪明，但是我不喜欢他。

4. 我喜欢这个包，因为它携带方便。

5. 我一听到这个消息就过来了。

6. 你必须在今晚 9 点前完成任务。

7. 直到今天我才知道有她这么个人。

8. 三年前，这家公司成立了。

9. 露西昨天没有来学校，因为她感冒了。

10. 她有空就会去当志愿者。

11. 他小时候就会弹钢琴了。

12. 入乡随俗。

13. 虽然我很尊敬他，但是我并不同意他的观点。

14. 只要你努力付出，你就会有所收获。

15. 他太累了，再也走不动了。

16. 无论你去哪里，都要照顾好自己。

17. 为了赚取生活费，他暑假去做兼职。

18. 如果明天下雨了，我就不去公园了。

19. 我比他高。

20. 如果你心情不好，就去运动吧。

扫一扫查看
练习参考答案

扫一扫查看
本章拓展资料

Unit 9

Forest Protection

💬 Learning Objectives

【About Knowledge】

1. To get to know how to protect the forests.

2. To master useful words and expressions about green living.

3. To talk about protecting the environment.

4. To know more about Non-finite Verbs.

【About Skills】

To know more about writing a Memo.

Section I *Dialogues*

📖 Dialogue 1

Protecting the Forests

Lucy is talking with her friend, Ryan, about forests protection in Tasmania.

Lucy: So, who are **some of** the people fighting to protect these trees **besides** you as an environmental scientist?

Ryan: Well, in Tasmania, the first green political party was developed, so yeah, they obviously want to **protect** the forests a lot, and they have big protests. They tie themselves to trees and sit up in trees to protect the trees.

Lucy: People actually still do that? Tie themselves to trees?

Ryan: Oh, every day in **Tasmania**. It's a big issue. A very big issue.

Lucy: I once heard of a girl who lived in a tree for a month because she wanted to stop the **deforestation** company or people from cutting down that tree, so she lived up there and she had people bring her supplies but she never came down.

Ryan: That happens in Tasmania as well. There're people today maybe up to fifty permanently living up in trees.

Lucy: Wow!

Ryan: Yeah, so. I don't know how they do it.

Lucy: That's kind of crazy…So, Ryan, from the company's point of view, playing the devil's **advocate** here, I think they **provide** jobs **for** all the people who are working to make trees into paper. What do you think they have to say about that?

Ryan: Well, it's true. They do provide jobs, and some cities, some small towns do rely on logging industry to provide jobs and support the shops in the place, but…

Lucy: But!

Ryan: But! Yeah. Tourism is a very big industry in Tasmania, and the logging industry may do harm to the tourism there as well, because it makes **certain** areas not useful for sight-seeing anymore, not very pretty.

Lucy: Yeah, you're right. If the whole forest is missing, I guess nobody would really want to go there.

Ryan: Yeah, there are some really beautiful spots in Tasmania which have been tarnished a little by **the logging industry**.

Vocabulary and notes

1. some of: 其中一些

2. besides: adv. as well or in addition；此外；而且；再说；以及

3. protect: v. to prevent somebody or something from being harmed or damaged；保护；防护；（制定法律）保护

4. Tasmania: state in southeastern Australia, occupying the island of Tasmania. First settled by the British in 1803, it became a separate colony in 1825.（大洋洲东南的）塔斯马尼亚岛

5. deforestation: n. the process of removing the trees from an area of land；毁林；滥伐森

林；烧林

6. advocate: v. to publicly support a particular policy or way of doing things；提倡；拥护；支持

7. provide…for: v. make ready, do what is necessary, for；为……作准备；为……提供

8. certain: adj. having no doubts about something；肯定；确定；确信；无疑

9. the logging industry: 伐木业

Dialogue 2

Protecting the Rainforest

Susan is sharing her visit to Tianjin rainforest botanical garden with her friend, David.

Susan: Today I went to visit the Tianjin **rainforest botanical garden**. It was really impressive.

David: Which part of the museum do you like best?

Susan: I like to visit the **micro** rainforest. There is a lot of vegetation I have never seen before, such as the king flower.

David: Yes, the rainforest is **undoubtedly** one of the most valuable resources given to all living things on earth. We can appreciate the dense broad-leaved forest, the giant python coiling in the trees, and study the exotic flowers and plants hidden in the jungle.

Susan: In the botanical garden, you can also participate in special **ethnic** festivals, such as the Dai People's "**Water Splashing Festival**".

David: What a great experience it was!

Susan: At the end of the visit, the staff told us that due to improper development and poor protection, the rainforest in many countries are being seriously damaged, and the area of tropical rainforest is decreasing at an alarming rate. What impact does this have on the environment?

David: I think that it will **affect** the global water cycle and balance, which will lead to the decrease of surface water, the weakening of water evaporation and transpiration, and the drying of air, which will **lead to** the decrease of precipitation, drought and even the imbalance of drought and flood. So the rainforest is really important.

Susan: At the same time, the **destruction** of tropical rainforest will increase the carbon dioxide content in the atmosphere, which will lead to the increase of temperature and global warming.

David: What's worse, the destruction of the rainforest will also lead to the mass extinction of rainforest species, resulting in the continuous reduction of biodiversity and bio-genetic genes.

Susan: To stop the rainforest from being destroyed, we should advocate reducing deforestation.

David: That's right. We can reduce the use of disposable chopsticks and toothpicks to protect more trees from being cut down.

Vocabulary and notes

1. rainforest botanical garden: 雨林植物园

2. micro: adj. very small；极小的；显微的

3. undoubtedly: adv. used for saying that something is certainly true or is accepted by everyone；无疑；毋庸置疑地

4. python: n. a very large snake that kills animals for food by wrapping itself around them and crushing them；蟒；蚺蛇

5. ethnic: adj. sharing distinctive cultural traits as a group in society；民族的；种族的；具有民族特色的；异国风味的

6. Water Splashing Festival: 泼水节

7. affect: v. to act upon or have an effect on somebody or something；影响；侵袭；假装；使感染

8. lead to: 导致；引起；通往

9. destruction: n. the act or process of destroying something；破坏；毁灭；摧毁

Dialogue 3

Green Living

Han lei is talking with his classmate, Li Ming, about green living to protect the environment.

Han Lei: What did you do over the weekend?

Li Ming: I attended a **global warming** rally in London. It was **fantastic** to meet so many people who care about the environment.

Han Lei: Do you think there's anything we can do to reverse the damage that's been done already?

Li Ming: It might not be possible to **fix** the problems that we've created, but there are lots of things we can do to avoid more damages.

Han Lei: Like what?

Li Ming: Well, we can use **public** transport instead of taking our cars **for a start**.

Han Lei: **What else** can we do to protect the environment?

Li Ming: If you do have to drive, you should make sure that your car runs on **unleaded** petrol. Besides, renewable energy is a good choice for domestic use.

Han Lei: How about recycling? Does that actually help?

Li Ming: Yes. You should take your glass, paper, plastic, cardboard, and tin cans to a **recycling** center.

Han Lei: What do you think is the biggest worry for our future?

Li Ming: I think that the issue of greatest concern is having enough sources of clean water for everyone.

Han Lei: I had no idea you were such an environmentalist before!

Li Ming: **To be honest**, in order for the earth to continue to be a habitable place, we have to become more responsible for the environment.

Vocabulary and notes

1. global warming: n. an increase in the world's temperatures, believed to be caused in part by the greenhouse effect；全球（气候）变暖；地球大气层变暖

2. fantastic: adj. extraordinarily good；极好的；了不起的；很大的

3. fix: v. to repair, mend, or correct something；修理；确定；安排；安装

4. public: adj. relating to or concerning the people at large or all members of a community；平民的；大众的；公众的；百姓的

5. for a start: used in an argument to indicate that you are making the first point of many；首先；正蠢蠢欲动；开始

6. what else: 还有什么呢

7. unleaded: adj. not containing tetraethyl lead as an antiknock additive and consequently

less harmful to the environment；无铅的；不含铅的

8. recycle: v. to process used or waste material so that it can be used again 回收；再循环；资源回收

9. to be honest: used when telling someone what you really think, especially when it may be something that they do not want to hear；老实说；说实话；说实在的

📖 Dialogue 4

Protecting the environment

Jenny, Kay and Mason are talking about how to protect the environment in the class discussion.

Jenny: Today I read a book. This book is about our **environment** which is now in danger.

Kay: Yes, once our environment was very beautiful. The air was fresh, the water was clean, the sky was blue, and so on.

Jenny: But today, everything is different. There are various **pollutions**. Factories in the towns and cities **drain** waste liquid to the lakes, rivers and seas. Waste gases and factories bring air pollution.

Kay: At the same time, people are killing more and more animals and some of them are **disappearing** from the Earth forever.

Mason: People are polluting the land, polluting the water, polluting the air! People should **immediately** take actions to stop the pollution. Let's get together to protect our environment.

Jenny: Everyone should make a **contribution** to protecting the environment. Taking care of our environment is very important. Wherever you live, you can do something around your **neighbourhood**.

Kay: It is our duty to keep our environment clean and tidy. We can do a lot of things to protect our environment.

Mason: Start from now, each and every one of us should not **litter** randomly, not spit everywhere.

Jenny: Love flowers; Protect the animals; Save water; Take good care of the resources.

Mason: Let us join hands together to protect our home!

Kay: I believe that our environment will become more beautiful. People's life will become better.

Vocabulary and notes

1. environment: n. all the external factors influencing the life and activities of people, plants, and animals；生态环境；自然环境

2. pollution: n. the state or condition of being polluted, or the presence of pollutants；污染；污染物；垃圾；玷污

3. drain: v. to flow out of something, often leaving it empty or dry, or allow a liquid to do this；排空；流出；（使）流光；放干

4. disappear: v. to go out of sight; to be impossible to find；消失；失踪；离开；绝迹

5. immediately: adv. without delay or without pausing beforehand；立即；马上；即刻；紧接

6. contribution: n. something such as money or time that is given, especially to a common fund or for a specific purpose；贡献；捐款；捐赠；稿件

7. neighbourhood: n. a local community with characteristics that distinguish it from the areas around it；街区；城区；（统称）某街区（或城区）的居民；所在地

8. litter: v. to make a place, especially a public place or the outdoors, untidy by leaving or scattering rubbish；乱扔；使乱七八糟；使凌乱；使遍布（一般指不好的东西）

Activity

Make up a dialogue based on the following situation.

Suppose you are a journalist in a seminar on global warming, you are having a conversation with an expert to talk about protecting the forests.

Section II Extensive Reading

Passage 1

Importance of Forests

Forests and **biodiversity** are key to all life forms. The richer the diversity of life, the greater the opportunity for medical **discoveries**, economic development and adaptive responses to such new challenges as climate change.

Below are some more importance of forests:

Watershed

Forests serve as a watershed. (A watershed: The area of land that contributes water to a stream or river. Watersheds come in all sizes—some are millions of square miles, while others are just a few acres.) This is because almost all water **ultimately** comes from rivers and lakes and from forest-derived water tables. Some rivers running through forests are also kept cool and from **drying out**. "The Amazon is by far the largest watershed and largest river system in the world occupying over 6 million square kilometers. Over two-thirds of all the freshwater found on Earth is in the Amazon Basin's rivers, streams, and tributaries."

Habitat and Ecosystems

Forests serve as a home (habitat) to millions of animals. Think of the many types of reptiles (snakes and lizards), wild animals and insects, birds and tree-top animals as well as all those that live in the forest **streams** and rivers.

Animals form part of the food chain in the forests. All these different animals and plants make up biodiversity, and the interaction with one another and with their physical environment is what we call an Ecosystem. Healthy **ecosystems** can better **withstand** and recover from **a variety of** disasters such as floods and wildfires.

Did you know...

In many developing countries more than 80% of total energy (fuel-wood and charcoal) consumed by people and industry is derived from forests. Trade in timber and other forest products is estimated at almost 330 billion US Dollars /year. Its value **multiplies** as it is processed into a range of products used globally every day. Uses of genetic diversity within forests enable the development of new medicines and progress in health care and science.

（来源：https://www.iucn.org/theme/forests）

Vocabulary and notes

1. biodiversity: n. the range of organisms present in a particular ecological community or system；生物多样性

2. discovery: n. something new that has been learned or found；发现；（剧情的）发展；显露；被发现的事物

3. watershed: n. an important period, time, event, or factor that marks a change or division；分水岭；转折点；分水线

4. ultimately: adv. after a process or activity has ended；最终；最后；归根结底；终究

5. dry out: 干透；使干；完全变干

6. stream: n. to flow, or appear to flow, continuously or quickly and in large quantities；流；溪；小河

7. ecosystem: n. a localized group of interdependent organisms together with the environment that they inhabit and depend on；生态系统

8. withstand: v. to be strong enough to stand up to somebody or remain unchanged by something such as extremes of heat or pressure；承受；经受住；抵住；顶住

9. a variety of: 各种各样的；多种多样的

10. multiply: v. to increase by a large amount；增多；增殖；（成倍）增加

11. Forests and biodiversity are key to all life forms. The richer the diversity of life, the greater the opportunity for medical discoveries, economic development and adaptive responses to such new challenges as climate change. 森林和生物多样性对所有生命来说都极其重要。生命的多样性越丰富，医学发现、经济发展和适应气候变化等新挑战的机会就越大。

12. This is because almost all water ultimately comes from rivers and lakes and from forest-derived water tables. 这是因为几乎所有的水最终都来自河流和湖泊以及森林衍生的地下水。

13. All these different animals and plants make up biodiversity, and the interaction with one another and with their physical environment is what we call an Ecosystem. 所有这些不同的动物和植物构成生物多样性，它们之间以及它们与自然环境的相互作用就是我们所说的生态系统。

 译文

森林的重要性

森林和生物多样性对所有生命来说都极其重要。生命的多样性越丰富，医学发现、经济发展和适应气候变化等新挑战的机会就越大。

以下是森林的其他几个重要功能：

分水岭

森林是分水岭。(分水岭:向溪流或河流供水的陆地区域。区域大小不一,有些面积数百万平方英里,而另一些只有几英亩。)这是因为几乎所有的水最终都来自河流和湖泊以及森林衍生的地下水。一些河流流经森林,能够局部受到冷却,也不至于干涸。"亚马孙河是迄今为止世界上最大的分水岭和最大的河流系统,占地600多万平方公里。地球上超过三分之二的淡水都存在于亚马孙流域的河流、溪流和支流中。"

栖息地和生态系统

森林是数百万动物的家园。想想许多种类的爬行动物(蛇和蜥蜴)、野生动物、昆虫、鸟类和树顶动物以及所有生活在森林溪流和河流中的动物。

动物是森林食物链的一部分。所有这些不同的动物和植物构成生物多样性,它们之间以及它们与自然环境的相互作用就是我们所说的生态系统。健康的生态系统能够更好地抵御洪水和火灾等各种灾害并从中恢复活力。

你知道吗……

在许多发展中国家,人类和工业消耗的总能源(燃料木材和木炭)的80%以上来自森林。木材和其他森林产品的贸易值估计约为3300亿美元/年。这些木材和其他森林产品被加工成一系列产品,供全球人口日常使用,它们的价值成倍增长。利用森林内的遗传多样性可以开发新的药物,并在保健和科学方面取得进展。

Passage 2

Primary forests: a priority nature-based solution

Primary forests are often the **customary** homelands of Indigenous Peoples(土著人民). They are essential to protecting cultural and linguistic diversity and fundamentally important to the **livelihoods** of local communities. They also provide a wide range of ecosystem services: protect the most **carbon** and biodiversity, produce the cleanest freshwater, regulate water flows, have local cooling effects and prevent erosion. And yet they are disappearing very fast. We lose millions of hectares of primary forest every year. We have lost a third of the planet's forest cover already, and less than a third of what remains is primary forest.

The message is simple. We are facing **accelerating** degradation of biodiversity and climate change crises. We cannot **resolve** either crisis without prioritizing the protection of primary forests and engaging in large-scale ecological restoration. This is critical to human well-being, to the diversity of life on Earth, and for a climate-safe future.

We know how to protect and restore ecosystem **integrity**: it requires **empowering** and supporting Indigenous Peoples（土著人民）and communities who are the traditional owners and stewards of these forests, and scaling up protected areas of all governance types, payments for ecosystem services, forest ecosystem connectivity **conservation** initiatives, and other effective area-based conservation measures. This will in turn require shifting funding from subsidies that fuel forest degradation and destruction to conservation-as well as greatly increasing the two percent of climate funding currently allocated to forests and **prioritizing** it appropriately, to support the highest impact climate mitigation actions: primary forest protection, afforestation（造林）and ecological restoration.

（来源：https://www.iucn.org/）

Vocabulary and notes

1. primary: adj. ranked as most important；主要的；最重要的；基本的；最初的

2. customary: adj. conforming to what is usual or normal；习俗的；习惯的；（某人）特有的

3. livelihood: n. something that provides income to live on, especially paid work；赚钱谋生的手段；生计

4. carbon: n. a chemical element that is found in all living things, and can also exist as diamonds or coal；碳；碳（指导致全球变暖的二氧化碳气体）

5. accelerate: v. to move increasingly quickly, or cause something to do this；加速；促进；速度增加

6. resolve: v. to come to a firm decision about something, or cause somebody to do this；决心；决定；解决（问题）

7. integrity: n. the state of being complete or undivided；完整；诚实正直；完好

8. empower: v. to give somebody power or authority；授权；使能

9. conservation: n. the keeping or protecting of something from change, loss, or damage；保护；保持；文物保护；（对自然环境的）保护

10. prioritize: v. to decide in what order you should do things, based on how important or urgent they are；给……排出先后顺序；给……优先权

11. They also provide a wide range of ecosystem services: they protect the most carbon and biodiversity, produce the cleanest freshwater, regulate water flows, have local cooling effects

and prevent erosion. 它们还提供广泛的生态系统服务：它们保护最多的碳和生物多样性，生产最清洁的淡水，调节水流，具有局部冷却作用和防止侵蚀。

12. We cannot resolve either crisis without prioritizing the protection of primary forests and engaging in large-scale ecological restoration. 如果不把保护原始森林放在优先地位，不进行大规模的生态恢复，我们就无法解决这两个危机。

13. This will in turn require shifting funding from subsidies that fuel forest degradation and destruction to conservation-as well as greatly increasing the two percent of climate funding currently allocated to forests and prioritizing it appropriately, to support the highest impact climate mitigation actions: primary forest protection, afforestation and ecological restoration. 反过来，原本投入的资金无意间助长的森林退化，破坏了森林，现在需要将这笔资金投入到新林养护上，并大大增加目前分配给森林的2%的气候资金，并对其进行适当的优先排序，以支持影响最大的气候减缓行动：原始森林保护，造林和生态恢复。

  译文

原始森林：基于自然的优先解决方案

　　原始森林往往是土著人民的传统家园，它对保护文化和语言多样性至关重要，也对当地社区人民的生计至关重要。它们还提供广泛的生态系统服务：它们保护数量最多的碳和生物多样性，生产最清洁的淡水，调节水流，具有局部冷却作用和防止侵蚀。但它们正在迅速消失。我们每年损失数百万公顷的原始森林。我们已经失去了地球上三分之一的森林，剩下的森林中原始森林所占比例不到三分之一。

　　这一现象所传递出的信息很明显。我们正面临着生物多样性加速退化和气候变化的危机。如果不把保护原始森林放在优先地位，不进行大规模的生态恢复，我们就无法解决这两个危机。这对人类福祉、地球生命多样性和气候安全的未来至关重要。

　　我们知道如何保护和恢复生态系统的完整性：这需要赋予土著人民和作为这些森林的传统所有者和管理者的社区以权力和支持，并扩大所有治理类型的保护区，支付生态系统服务费，实施森林生态系统连通性保护倡议，以及其他有效的区域保护措施。反过来，原本投入的资金无意间助长的森林退化，破坏了森林，现在需要将这笔资金投入到新林养护上，并大大增加目前分配给森林的2%的气候资金，并对其进行适当的优先排序，以支持影响最大的气候减缓行动：原始森林保护，造林和生态恢复。

Section III Case Analysis in Intercultural Communication

Frequent Bowing

As a Chinese student, I had the honor to go to Kyoto University for exchange study. Although it was only a few days, I still felt the cross-cultural maladjustment（不适应）. The most impressive one was the bow ceremony of Japan.

In class, teachers respect students very much and will give us a bow back. I go to the supermarket to do some shopping and have a meal. The salesmen and waiters will bow when they meet. Different from the Chinese people's slight greeting, the Japanese bow ceremony is much more complicated. They will take different degrees of bowing according to different occasions and different meanings. Out of politeness, I often "bow back", but this makes me very unaccustomed, and also very tired. It can be said that in Japan, bowing is a very common and popular way of communication. But in China, only in special occasions people bow, and usually the weaker side of the power relationship bows to the stronger side, such as students bow to teachers, children bow to parents and so on.

It reminds me of a news story a few years ago. During his visit to Japan in 2009, Obama bowed to the emperor of Japan for nearly 90 degrees, which incurred criticism from the US media and conservatives. They accused Obama of behaving inappropriately as head of state, "belittling the power and dignity of the United States", violating the American etiquette tradition, looking "humble" and "kowtowing" to the emperor of Japan. The White House explained that it was out of respect for traditional Japanese customs and showed the president's courtesy. Perhaps because of pressure, when Obama met with the emperor of Japan again in 2014, he simply shook hands and did not "bow".

Questions for discussion

Why do Japanese bows? Should we bow in Japan?

分析：日本鞠躬礼的复杂程度要高于中国，文化内涵也比中国丰富。日本是一个十分注重礼仪的国家，在生活中随时可见人们之间相互鞠躬。对日本人而言，这不仅是一种日常礼节，而且是一种生活方式，一种文化内涵，隐含了日本人民的精神特质。日本和中国一样，讲究人际关系的和谐，鞠躬礼仪就是维护人际关系和谐的重要方式之一。日本的鞠躬礼具有标准的规范，会根据对象和场合的不同使用不同的鞠躬动作，这不仅表达了对对方的尊敬，也是自身良好修养的体现。日本同时还是一个注重社会等级的国家，晚辈要向长辈鞠躬、社会地位低的人要向社会地位高的人鞠躬，鞠躬正是等级观念的外在表现。

奥巴马在会见日本天皇时入乡随俗，主动向年事已高的日本天皇鞠躬，从跨文化交际角度来看，这是个非常聪明的交际策略，不仅显示了奥巴马作为一个大国总统对于他国文化的尊重，也体现了奥巴马自身的风度和魅力。在跨文化交际中，文化差异是不可避免的，关键是要去自觉尊重和了解他文化，采取"文化相对主义"的积极态度，不能用一种文化价值观作为判断一切的标准。

Section IV Practical Writing: Memo

Memo 是单词 Memorandum 的缩写，作为一种非正式的公文形式，备忘录是在单位内部为发放通知、联系工作、管理有关工作人员或下级部门对上级部门所使用的一种简短书面交流形式。

备忘录通常用于以下目的：
（1）告知决策；
（2）要求采取行动、作出回应；
（3）提醒安排、规则；
（4）提供建议。

备忘录的格式一般采用以下形式：
（1）上端的中间写上标题 Memorandum 或 Memo。
（2）To：收阅人的姓名或者职务，可以免除头衔和称谓。
（3）From：写发文人的姓名。一般情况下可以免写职务，免称谓。
（4）Date：日期，写在信笺的右上角或左边排列当中。
（5）Subject（主题）：用简短的语言对备忘录的内容进行概括。
（6）Body（正文）：备忘录可以免称呼，免客套用语。语言简洁明了，篇幅短小精悍，常用非正式用语。
（7）Reference Initials（经手人代号或姓名缩写）：撰写人姓名首字母，如 JM 等。

备忘录写作注意事项：
（1）书端部分包括发文机关的名称、地址、发文日期，有的还包括电报挂号、电传号、电话号码等。许多机关有自己特制的信笺，在写书端时，其格式和标点符号的使用与一般信件的相同。

（2）称呼从左边顶格写起，对一般机关、团体的负责人一般用 Dear Sir，对政府官员可用 Sir。

（3）正文、结束语和署名等项与一般信件的格式相同。"事因"一项目前采用得较少。

Sample

Memo

To: All students

From: Mr. Chen

Date: July 4. 2010

Subject: The class discipline

All the students should have the evening class from 7 p.m.to 8 p.m. from Mondays to Fridays. No one should be absent. Anyone who asks for leave should call Mr. Wang in advance.

If there is any questions, please consult the Dean Office.

Practice

Suppose you are to send a memo for the personnel manager to all staff on the May Day Holiday, which starts at 4:30 p.m. on the 30th April and ends at 9:00 a.m. on the third May. Now draft the memo.

Practice

Memo

Section V Grammar: Non-finite Verb（非谓语动词）

非谓语动词包括不定式、动名词、分词三种形式，非谓语动词在句子中不能单独作谓语，没有人称和数的变化，但仍保留动词的某些特征，如可以有自己的宾语、状语等。非谓语动词的否定形式在前面加 not。

一、动名词

动名词由动词的 -ing 形式构成，与现在分词同形。动名词既具有动词的特征，也具有名词的特征，在句中可作主语、表语、宾语等。

动名词保留着动词的特征，有时态和语态变化。其时态和语态形式如下表所示：

时态形式 语态形式	主动形式	被动形式
一般式	doing	being done
完成式	having done	having been done

1. 动名词的一般式和完成式的用法区别

动名词的一般式可以表示经常发生的动作，也可以表示与谓语动作同时发生或发生在谓语动作之前或之后的动作；而动名词的完成式一般表示动名词的动作是发生在谓语动词之前的动作。

例：Going to bed early is a good habit. 早睡是好习惯。（没有明确的时间）

例：He apologized for having broken his promise. 他因未遵守诺言表示道歉。

2. 动名词的被动式

动名词的逻辑主语是动名词所表示的动作的承受者时，动名词用被动形式。

例：I hate being cheated in office. 我痛恨在办公室被别人欺骗。（我和 cheat 是逻辑上的被动关系）

3. 动名词的句法功能

动名词相当于名词，在句中主要作主语、表语、宾语、定语等。

例：Finding a job is difficult these days. 现在找工作不容易。（作主语）

例：My hobby is singing. 我的爱好是唱歌。（作表语）

例：Would you mind opening the door? 劳驾把门打开好吗？（作宾语）

例：He insisted on giving up smoking. 他坚持戒烟。（作介词宾语）

Give a thief rope enough and he will hang himself. 多行不义必自毙。

例：He built a swimming pool in his garden. 他在花园建了一个游泳池。（作定语）

接动名词作宾语的动词有：

advise 建议	admit 承认	avoid 避免	allow 允许
bear 忍受	cannot help 禁不住	consider 考虑	delay 推迟
enjoy 喜欢	finish 完成	give up 放弃	imagine 想象
include 包括	keep 保持	keep on 持续	mind 介意
miss 错过	put off 推迟	practise 练习	permit 允许
resist 抵抗	risk 冒险	suggest 建议	stand 忍受

4. 动名词的逻辑主语

当动名词的逻辑主语与句子的主语不一致时，要在动名词前加上动名词的逻辑主语，构成了动名词的复合结构。动名词的逻辑主语一般是形容词性物主代词或名词所有格形式，但有时也可用人称代词宾格或名词的普通格。

例：Her coming to help encouraged me. 她来帮忙鼓舞了我。

例：Would you mind my /me using your telephone? 我能借用一下你的电话吗？

二、不定式

不定式的构成形式是 to +v. 原型，一种是带 to 的不定式（有 to 不定式）；一种是不带 to 的不定式（无 to 不定式）。在句中起着名词、形容词或副词的作用。不定式表动作，有以下形式：

语态形式 时态形式	主动形式	被动形式
一般式	to do	to be done
完成式	to have done	to have been done
进行式	to be doing	

1. 不定式的一般式、完成式和进行式的区别

例：I'm pleased to see you here. 很高兴在这里见到你。

例：I'm sorry to have kept you waiting so long. 真对不起让你等了这么长时间。

例：Mary pretended to be reading books when the teacher came in. 老师进来时，玛丽假装在读书。

2. 不定式的被动形式

当动词不定式的逻辑主语是不定式所表示的动作的承受者时，一般要用其被动形式例：The bike needs to be repaired. 自行车需要修理。

例：The floor seems to have been cleaned. 似乎有人打扫过地板。

3. 不定式的句法功能

不定式相当于名词、形容词、副词，因此在句中可作主语、宾语、表语、补足语、定语和状语等。

例：To live in China is Mr Smith's dream. (= It is Mr Smith's dream to live in China.) 生活在中国是史密斯先生的梦想。

例：I have decided to study computer science. 我决定学计算机科学。

例：My goal is to be a teacher. 我的目标是当一名教师。

例：Teachers want their students to develop fully. 老师们想让学生全面发展。

例：He was the first guest to arrive. 他是第一个来的客人。

例：She was surprised to see George walk in. 看到乔治进来，她很惊讶。

常见接不定式作宾语的动词有：

agree 同意	afford 负担得起	ask 要求	choose 选择
decide 决定	demand 要求	desire 要求	expect 期望
fail 失败	hope 希望	intend 打算	learn 学习
manage 设法做到	mean 打算	offer 主动提出	prepare 准备
pretend 假装	promise 许诺	refuse 拒绝	wish 希望

ask, want, wish, order, tell, persuade, advise, allow, warn, encourage, cause, require 等动词常用带 to 的不定式作补足语。

see, watch, hear, feel, notice, observe, look at, listen to, make, let, have 等动词常用省略 to 的不定式作补足语。

三、分词

分词有现在分词和过去分词两种。现在分词由动词加 -ing 形式构成，过去分词有规则和不规则之分，规则动词的过去分词由原形动词后加 -ed 构成，不规则动词的过去分词需单独记忆。分词保留了动词的特征，在句中可有自己的状语、逻辑主语和宾语，分词的否定形式是在前加 not。

1. 现在分词的一般式和完成式区别

例：We walked along the river bank, talking and laughing. 我们沿着河岸有说有笑地走着。（现在分词的一般式表示动作与谓语动作同时发生）

例：Having finished the work, she got ready to go home. 完成工作后，她准备回家。（现在分词的完成式表示动作发生在谓语动作之前）

2. 分词的句法功能

分词短语相当于形容词，在句中可以作定语（详见第七单元定语从句）、补足语和状语。如：an interesting book 一本有趣的书；a broken cup 一个破杯子。

例：I find this film very interesting. 我发现这部电影非常有趣。（形容词性质的分词作宾语补足话）

例：I see him passing by a bank. 我看见他正经过一家银行。（具有动作性质的现在分词作宾语补足语）

* **试比较以下句子，找出分词短语作后置定语和定语从句的关联：**

例：The man sitting by the window is my best friends.（分词短语作后置定语）

The man who is sitting by the window is my best friends.（定语从句）

坐在窗边的那名男子是我最好的朋友。

* **试比较以下句子，找出分词短语作状语和状语从句的关联：**

例：Hearing the news, they all jumped for joy.（分词短语作状语）

When they heard the news, they all jumped for joy.（状语从句）

听到这个消息，他们都高兴得跳了起来。

例：Not knowing her address or phone number, we couldn't get in touch with her.（分词短语作状语）

Because we didn't know her address or phone number, we couldn't get in touch with her.（状语从句）

由于不知道她的地址和电话号码，我们无法与她取得联系。

例：We walked along the river bank, talking and laughing.（分词短语作状语）

We walked along the river bank, talked and laughed.（状语从句）

我们沿着河岸有说有笑地走着。

例：Given enough money, we can carry out the project better.（分词短语作状语）

If we are given enough money, we can carry out the project better.（状语从句）

如果给予足够的资金，我们会把这个项目做得更好。

Exercise 1: Non-finite Verb（非谓语动词）

一、单项选择

1. I heard my neighbor _____ when I passed her window.

    A. cry
    B. to cry
    C. crying
    D. cried

2. Sadly, I'm fired and have no money and no place _____.

    A. live in
    B. to live
    C. living in
    D. to live in

3. The lady had difficulty _____ her luggage.

    A. carry
    B. to carry
    C. carrying
    D. carried

4. My brother is independent and he doesn't mind _____ alone at home.

    A. being left
    B. leaving
    C. to be left
    D. to leave

5. How about _____ to a concert?

    A. go
    B. goes
    C. going
    D. to go

6. _____ the news of the outbreak of the COVID-19, he made his mind to go to the front line.

    A. While hearing
    B. On hearing
    C. Having heard
    D. After hearing

7. Stop _____. This is a public place and smoking is not allowed here.

    A. smoke
    B. to smoke
    C. smokes
    D. smoking

8. She told her son _____ on the road.

    A. not play
    B. not plays
    C. not to play
    D. not playing

9. He will spend a large fortune _____ her a ring.

    A. been bought
    B. to buy
    C. buying
    D. bought

Good news goes on crutches. 好事不出门。

10. You'd better _____ too much time chatting online.

A. to not spend   B. not to spend

C. don't spend   D. not spend

11. My grandmother kept _____ stories to me at night when I was a child.

A. saying   B. telling

C. to tell   D. to say

12. — What's wrong with you?

    — I have some trouble _____ the answer.

A. to find   B. finding

C. find   D. found

13. _____ to the music is a good form of relaxation for the young today.

A. Listen   B. Listening

C. To listen   D. Listened

14. — Could you _____ down the radio please?

    — Grandpa is sleeping in the next room.

A. turning   B. to turn

C. turned   D. turn

15. We agreed _____ here but so far she hasn't turned up yet.

A. to meet   B. meeting

C. having met   D. to have met

16. Kids have fun _____ with sand on the beach.

A. play   B. to play

C. playing   D. played

17. Lucy's father asked her _____ the flower after supper.

A. to water   B. water

C. water   D. watered

18. My watch can't work. I need to have it _____ tomorrow.

A. repairing   B. to repair

C. repair   D. repaired

19. Could you tell me where _____ the bank?

A. how to find   B. can I find

C. to find D. find

20. She buries herself in _____ letters upstairs.

A. writing B. is writing

C. write D. writes

二、用所给词的适当形式填空

1. The teacher raised his voice to make himself _____ (hear).

2. _____ (have) no money, he tries his best to land a job.

3. He is looking at me _____ (smile).

4. _____ (see) is believing.

5. I forgot _____ (turn) off the light when I left the office.

6. I remember _____ (lock) the door yesterday when I left the room.

7. Tom opened the window _____ (breath) fresh air.

8. We saw him _____ (play) basketball on the playground yesterday.

9. _____ (finish) the task on time, I will ask my colleagues for help.

10. Lily sits there _____ (think) about what to eat.

11. Would you mind _____ (lend) me your dictionary?

12. I had my hair _____ (cut) this morning.

13. Children like _____ (eat) candies.

14. When I entered the room, I saw my sister _____ (eat) an apple.

15. _____ (learn) English by yourself is not an easy task.

16. It's time _____ (go) to bed.

17. Not _____ (receive) a reply, he turned around and left the conference room (会议室).

18. _____ (help) others is helping yourself.

19. It's important for us _____ (learn) math well.

20. You'd better _____ (bring) with you your coat because it can be cold at night in the mountain.

三、翻译

1. 他站在舞台上开心地笑着。

2. 我有很多话想跟你说。

3. 她每天都花三个小时学习英语。

4. 我忘了告诉她我已经看过这部电影了。

5. 我和露西来上海参加会议。

6. 不要再说话了，上课了。

7. 我想当一名志愿者。

8. 保护环境是我们每个人的责任。

9. 你最好把烟戒了，它对你身体不好。

10. 保持好心情非常重要。

11. 她忙于写书。

12. 我们同意在三个月内搬出这里。

13. 我听到她在弹钢琴。

14. 昨天我们班来了一位叫汤姆的男孩。

15. 从我家到公司要走半个小时。

16. 妈妈想给我买一台钢琴。

17. 他站在角落里不知道要干嘛。

18. 我室友经常让我教他数学。

19. 请记得遵守诺言。

20. 我喜欢在海边散步。

扫一扫查看
练习参考答案

扫一扫查看
本章拓展资料

参考文献
REFERENCES

[1] 汪福祥，马登阁. 文化撞击——案例评析［M］. 北京：石油出版社，1999.

[2] 朱勇. 跨文化交际案例与分析［M］. 北京：高等教育出版社，2018.

[3] 张道真. 张道真实用英语语法（新版）［M］. 北京：外语教学与研究出版社，2002.

[4] 张道真. 张道真英语语法大全练习册［M］. 北京：世界图书出版公司，2019.

[5] Pinho, Sofia A. Intercomprhension: A portal to teachers' intercultural sensitivity［J］. Language learning Journal, 2015, 43（2）:148-164.

[6] King, P. M., Baxter Magolda, M. B.. A developmental model of intercultural maturity［J］. Journal of College Student Development, 2005, 46:571-592.